When Your
Children
Hurt

OTHER BOOKS BY CHARLES STANLEY

When Your
Children
Hurt

Charles Stanley

THOMAS NELSON
Since 1798

NASHVILLE   DALLAS   MEXICO CITY   RIO DE JANEIRO   BEIJING

Published in Nashville, Tennessee, by Thomas Nelson. Thomas Nelson is a registered trademark of Thomas Nelson, Inc.

Thomas Nelson, Inc., titles may be purchased in bulk for educational, business, fund-raising, or sales promotional use. For information, please e-mail: SpecialMarkets@ThomasNelson.com.

Library of Congress Cataloging-in-Publication Data

Stanley, Charles.
    When your children hurt / by Charles Stanley.
      p. cm.
    Summary: "Dr. Charles Stanley digs deep into the truth of God's Word to dispel feelings such as guilt, denial, anger, and unforgiveness that arise when a child suffers"—Provided by publisher.
    ISBN: 978-1-4002-0098-6 (tradepaper)
    1. Parenting—Religious aspects—Christianity. 2. Emotions in children—Religious aspects—Christianity. 3. Suffering—Religious aspects—Christianity. 4. Children—Religious life. I. Title.
BV4529.S795 2008
248.8'45–dc22

2007041213

Printed in the United States of America

08 09 10 11 RRD 5 4 3 2 1

Call upon Me, and I will answer [you];
I will be with [you] in trouble.
Psalm 91:15 NASB

CONTENTS

The Heart's Cry

For years, I have watched, listened, and counseled people who have had to deal with all kinds of heartache and emotional pain. Some of the most difficult problems to understand have been in the area of suffering, especially involving children. While this is a book written to address this particular subject, the principles within these pages are taken from a lifetime of experience in the area of adversity. Therefore, they can be applied to the life of anyone who is struggling and longs to have hope and experience freedom from the bondage of worry and fear. You may be dealing with a tragedy so great and severe that you do not think you can cope another day. It may be that your son or daughter is fighting for his or her life. Some uncontrollable disease has taken over, and unless there is a miracle, the end will come quickly. You have prayed, looked for an answer, and turned up nothing on your own. Doctors persist in trying one new medication after another, but nothing seems to work. The look on your child's face breaks your heart, and you would give anything to turn back the hands of time, change the circumstances, and relive the joy that seems to have escaped your life and the lives of those in your family.

Or it could be that you have just received the news that your child has left home. He is addicted to drugs or alcohol or some other perverse activity. Anger fills your heart, but you also know that there has to be a horrendous struggle going on within his life. The battle with guilt rages, and you wonder why God has allowed this to happen. You were a good Mom, a loving Dad.

When our children hurt, we hurt too. We hurt because we want to ease the pain they are feeling. Or because we want to fix the situation—fast. From a human perspective, the stress we feel may grow even harder to handle at the thought of God allowing it to continue for a longer period of time than we would choose. The cry of our hearts is one of agony, and yet we know by reading God's Word that He has a plan for our suffering and for the hurt our children feel. In Psalm 34, David wrote, "The LORD is near to the brokenhearted and saves those who are crushed in spirit" (v. 18 NASB). This is God's encouragement to us. He understands our frustration when we battle something that appears to be far too much for us to handle. He also knows the outcome, and He also knows that we cannot carry the burden alone. This is the reason He has given us Himself. He is our comforter, our guide, our hope, and our strength. Nothing is too great for Him to handle, but we must come to a point where we realize that we need Him and we can do nothing apart from Him.

Each one of the people who came to Jesus seeking healing for their son or daughter came to this realization. Most had tried everything available to relieve the suffering of their child and nothing had worked. Jesus told one father, whose son had suffered a very long time, "'All things are possible to him who believes.' Immediately the boy's father cried out and said, 'I do believe; help my unbelief'" (Mark 9:23, 24 NASB). This may be your cry too: "Lord, I do believe; help my unbelief." If it is, then believe that God has heard your cry, and He will answer. He may lead you along a straight path that moves quickly or one that seems to travel on and on. Regardless of the way, always remember that He has a plan and He will never leave you alone. I want to challenge you to trust Him and allow Him to work fully and completely in your life and the lives of your children. God has His best in mind even when the pain seems unbearable (Rom. 8:28). He knows the road of affliction is long and difficult to walk. He understands your feelings of fear and frustration. The tears you cry are ones He has wept as well. He is your Savior, and the light of hope you long to have is found in His gracious, awesome presence.

CHAPTER 1

He Never Asked Why

"My son never really asked why this happened to him," the mother commented. "But I sure did. On more than one occasion, I asked God, 'Why? Why would You allow this to happen to such a sweet boy—a boy who was not disobedient or hung around with the wrong crowd?' He was full of life—fifteen years old and ready to begin learning how to drive. That's when everything began to unravel."

Several years into the long-term illness of her son, this mother's world was still unraveling, but the process now included a troubled marriage and a daughter who was struggling to become a woman. When a child is seriously sick, the entire family feels the weight of the burden. And when a child remains sick for a long period of time, the pressure that comes with the experience can build to a point of serious explosion.

ONE WOMAN'S STORY

The woman across from me looked up with eyes full of sadness as she remembered that painful time, but also they contained a strong sense of hope. However, a few years ago this would not have been the case. Her son, who had appeared to be normal and healthy, suddenly collapsed with a seizure. "One minute he was at a friend's house talking and being a normal kid, and the next moment he was lying on the floor physically contorted." When she received the news, everyone tried to reassure her that everything was fine. It was just an accident—maybe the result of a playful blow to the head; but deep inside she felt uneasy. Her maternal intuition told her differently, and over the days and months that followed, she was right.

"When I finally accepted the fact that we were looking at a serious problem, my husband and I agreed that we would have to trust the doctors completely. We jumped from the shock of having a healthy son to facing a possible serious illness without taking time to consider God. We were young in our faith and probably not aware of how to handle adversity like this. It was simple to trust God with things like a car repair or a shift in our jobs, but neither one of us had ever faced something with such strong potential—potential for good, but mostly from our perspective, potential for bad."

While I'm not a Christian psychologist, I have certainly talked to enough friends in this field to know that when our children hurt, we, as parents, hurt to an even greater degree. One of the greatest challenges this woman faced was to let go of her personal expectations. "I kept asking myself, 'How can I fix this? Where can I go for help?' I wanted a solution to the problem and I didn't want to wait, but waiting is exactly what we had to do, and for a long stretch of time it seemed that we were waiting from one episode to another. Always fighting feelings in the back of our minds that the next one could be the one that ended my son's life, we prayed, but our prayers were not focused on God or discovering His purpose for this suffering. They were directed toward finding the right doctor with the right plan. And we were not about to accept 'wait' as an answer to our prayers."

Most parents and loved ones who have watched children suffer take this approach. It is not unusual, but usually it is not effective when it comes to finding the answers to the questions we have regarding the trials of life. I believe "Why?" is the number one question every parent asks when the child he or she loves is struggling with a physical, emotional, or mental illness. Job could handle the loss of his material possessions. However, when his servant came and told him that his children had died, he stood up and "tore his robe and shaved his head, and he fell to the ground and worshiped" (Job 1:19, 20 NASB). When we speak of adversity, we are talking about all kinds of opposition, tribulation, trials, heartaches, burdens, afflictions, and suffering.

My friend continued to tell her story—one that was full of frustration, especially in the early stages of her son's illness. "The first doctor ran a few tests and tried to reassure us that what our son experienced may have been a fluke. I wasn't so convinced. My mind wanted to accept his reasoning, but deep in my heart I knew differently. When we were faced with another seizure and then another one, I knew something was wrong, and I had to find what the answer was to the puzzle that was forming in front of me. This is when we began going from one doctor to another. I was on a mission: find the answer to my son's suffering. I took the message of Matthew 7:7, 8 NASB seriously: "Ask, and it will be given to you; seek, and you will find; knock, and it will be opened to you. For everyone who asks receives, and he who seeks finds, and to him who knocks it will be opened." I was going to knock on every door possible to find out why my son was sick. During this time, I continued to pray and tell the Lord that I was determined to trust Him and would never deny His love for us. But that was what I called a surface discussion with God, because deep inside I knew that I had not come to a point where I was willing to be still and listen to what God wanted to say to me.

"As the seizures increased, so did my tenacity. We tried different medications, different forms of treatments, and different means of evaluation. This was before the MRI was used on a regular basis. Finally, when it seemed we were at the end of our rope, a neurologist cut off our final thread of hope with a series of words that sent our world crashing into unbearable reality. He looked at me and my husband and said, 'You need to accept the fact that your son has epilepsy and move on.' He packed us off with a handful of prescriptions and nothing else. Sure, we could and did turn to Christian counselors for support, but something inside of me said there was hope—keep your hope alive. Then one day, I realized that a deep spiritual chasm stood between us and the hope we longed to have.

"Little did we know the journey we were about to undertake would span over several years and take countless twists and turns. It was amazing to me that through all of this, my son never asked, 'Why me?' He suffered, he hurt, and he had to deal with the fact that his entire life had been placed on semi-hold. He could not get his driver's license because we never knew if he would have a seizure. He could not agree to work on certain part-time jobs because he might go into a blank stare—something that began as the seizures increased."

Adversity comes in different sizes, shapes, forms, and intensity. Some parents sincerely believe that they can shield their children from ever experiencing the difficulties of life, but this is just not true. God allows heartache to touch our lives for a purpose. There is something tremendously valuable He wants us to learn through the process of suffering. Trying to prevent a loved one from experiencing a serious illness or trial is futile and can have devastating results. Likewise, being careless with our advice, guidance, and actions can be just as deadly. God provides the right sense of balance, but we must be willing to stop and honestly deal with our anxious thoughts.

THE SOURCE OF ADVERSITY

When trouble strikes, one of the first things we do is stop and think, *What have I done to cause this? Why has this happened? Who's to blame?* This may seem like a normal reaction and it is for a normal person, but God wants us to live above the normal and average response and attitude of this world. I remember once hearing an executive ask, "Who do I blame for this horrible mistake?" We cannot play the "blame game" and truly live the abundant life that God has for us to experience. We may have to face horrendous suffering, but blaming others for careless acts and thoughtless deeds only leads to bitterness, isolation, and depression. You may be in a situation where your son or daughter is suffering due to something someone else has done. You have a choice to make, and you must consider it carefully: either you can continue to seek retribution or you can release the individual into God's care. Notice I did not say anything about a lack of accountability.

God holds each one of us accountable for our actions. But He also tells us, "Vengeance is Mine, and retribution, in due time their foot will slip; for the day of their calamity is near, and the impending things are hastening upon them" (Deut. 32:35 NASB). Though we are armed with this verse, God does not want us to carry it around in our hearts as if it is a well-sharpened weapon. Instead, He calls us to roll the burden of our hearts—our grief and sorrow—over onto Him. He is our burden bearer. Nothing is too difficult or heavy for Him to bear. Leave your

He Never Asked Why

sorrow at the foot of His cross and allow Him to set your heart free from every thought of unforgiveness. If you don't, you will carry it with you the rest of your days.

Over my years as a pastor, I have encountered people who simply do not want to be free from the anger they have stowed away in their hearts. At first, the frustration they felt was nothing more than a smoldering fire. Anger is a normal part of the grief process that most people have to work through. If left unattended, it will become a smoldering fire that quickly will turn into a wildfire burning out of control. And once it does, all it leaves behind are charred remains of hope. There is never a reason to give up. I have seen people come through the most difficult of circumstances, but the way they did this was God's way and not their way. Will you take the first step of faith and admit that you need God's help? If you cannot go any further than this right now, then it is enough.

Only One Issue Is Important

Once the initial shock of the illness settled in, this mother and her husband fell into an all too familiar pattern. They began asking, "Lord, is my son's illness the result of something we have done?" These parents searched through the mental files of their lives looking for evidence that would tell them why this had happened. They were hoping that if they confessed enough wrong actions, God would hear their prayers and heal their son, but He does not work this way. He is not a God of wrath. Yes, there are consequences to sin, but the Lord is not in heaven looking down and waiting for us to make a wrong move so He can punish us. Accidents happen. Problems arise. Serious illnesses attack even the most loving people. We live in a fallen world, and sickness is a part of this broken state.

Somehow when innocent children are involved, it makes the illness or the injury, and the sorrow that accompanies it, all the more difficult to bear. We can justify hurt if it comes to someone we feel deserves it, but not if it comes to a young person—someone whose life has just begun. We don't have a prescription for that in our heart files. However, as you read on, you will discover what this mother learned about God: He is truly faithful all the time, in every situation, and without fail He has a plan for our suffering and the suffering of our loved one. There are two important points that we need to know up front about adversity:

1. It can be the greatest means of maturing and growing us up in our Christian walk with the Lord, or it can become a slippery avenue to discouragement.

2. The source of the adversity, as bad as it may seem, is not the issue. No matter how painful it is to watch your loved ones suffer, the trial should not become your central focus. Instead, your *reaction* to the problem or sorrow is the most important thing. If you respond properly, you

will sense God's closeness, understanding, and blessing. If you respond with feelings of anger and rebellion, you will experience a deep sense of loss and emptiness.

God does not provide the sense of peace we need to endure hardships if we are intent on fighting against Him. If we continue along this path, we will feel the weight of the emotional burden as it grows. He never intends for us to handle the problems of life alone. He knows that we cannot successfully bear up under the pressure without His help. He created us to need Him—His guidance, wisdom, reassurance, and peace. But like the woman whose story we are following, many times we sincerely believe that if we force the issue with God—press Him for an answer—He will relent, cave in to our demands, and give us what we want. God doesn't work that way. He is sovereign, and though it is difficult to watch our children and other loved ones suffer and struggle with the issues of life, we must learn that God has a plan for the suffering and we need to submit to it to gain relief.

"We did not understand until much later," the woman admitted, "that the prayers we had been praying were small prayers—prayers to get us to the right doctor with the solution to our problem. They were not prayers of faith—simple or otherwise. Oh, we had faith, but it was not until the end of our odyssey that I realized the true nature of faith that God desired for us."

There are times when God is moved to action by the words of our prayers, but His movement has nothing to do with our demands and everything to do with His timing. In other words, our prayers do not change God's plans or purposes. If they did, He would not be sovereign. God uses prayer to change us. It alters the way we view our circumstances by teaching us to focus on Him and not on ourselves. God knows exactly what He is after in our lives, and He will accomplish it. The woman continued by saying, "I remember my husband and I became so bent on finding a cure for my son's seizures that one time we drove five hundred miles to see a doctor, who did not know us and we had never met. We were just so desperate. We knew we had to keep trying. God allowed us to do this. I guess He must have been waiting for us to either turn to Him or run out of fuel. But in my mind, I was just getting started."

ONLY BELIEVE!

We do not have the privilege of walking out on the will of God even when His will includes pain, disappointment, and severe trials. I remember once a young father, who had lost his son in a terrible accident, asking me, "How can this be God's will for my life? It doesn't make sense." In my heart, I admitted that it did not make sense to me either. I thought of my own children and wondered how I would cope should something unthinkable happen to one of them. Nothing touches a parent's heart like the news of someone else's child having to battle cancer or suffering from some injustice done to them. The unthinkable is just that—something we never want to consider. And yet it does happen.

Jairus was an official in the synagogue. This meant he was

responsible for the services held there. He also would have been one of the men who made sure the synagogue was clean. This point becomes very important as his story unfolds:

> As Jesus returned, the people welcomed Him, for they had all been waiting for Him. And there came a man named Jairus . . . and he fell at Jesus' feet, and began to implore Him to come to his house; for he had an only daughter, about twelve years old, and she was dying. But as He went, the crowds were pressing against Him. And a woman who had a hemorrhage for twelve years, and could not be healed by anyone, came up behind Him and touched the fringe of His cloak, and immediately her hemorrhage stopped. (Luke 8:40–44 NASB)

Though Jairus probably did not realize that anything had happened, he was to find out shortly. Suddenly, the Savior stopped, along with everyone with Him. Someone had touched Him, and He felt the healing power of God go out of Him. It did not just leave Him. It moved, rushed from Him to the object of faith that now lay at His feet—a woman whose life had been characterized by misery, rejection, isolation, and uncleanness. We can imagine Jairus's gasp. The one Person he believed could heal his daughter—his only child—was being delayed!

Have you ever thought, *If only I could talk to this one person or see this certain doctor, then I know my loved one—my child—would get better.* These were probably Jairus's thoughts.

He had to lay aside the fact that he was a Jewish official. Most men in his position did not believe in Jesus or the healing work He was doing. But Jairus was desperate. This was his only child and a daughter he loved greatly. If necessary, he would deny his religious occupation to seek Jesus' help. He had seen how the Savior had healed others, and like any loving father, he wanted the same for his little girl.

As they were going to Jairus's home, Jesus stopped to heal a woman (Luke 8:47, 48). As the scene unfolded, Jairus had to do several things:

He had to wait.

He had to calculate the cost. As a synagogue official, he knew the Man who was willing to go home with him was now considered spiritually unclean.

He had to seize the opportunity to learn from the situation. Jesus had planned it this way. Jairus had humbled himself, but that was a simple first step. Now, God was requiring him to take an even greater step of faith by trusting the fact that Jesus was the only One who could satisfy his greatest need.

As they were about to resume their journey, a man from Jairus's household arrived with horrifying news: "Your daughter has died; do not trouble the Teacher anymore" (Luke 8:49 NASB). Jesus knew what Jairus was feeling and said, "Do not be afraid any longer; only believe, and she will be made well" (v. 50 NASB). There was no other recorded discussion between them. Jairus had to make a serious decision:

- Trust his feelings, which were fear-based, or
- Trust the Savior, even though all the physical evidence concerning his daughter's well-being seemed to go against all rational thought and belief.

When it seemed that there was no hope, Jesus had turned to him and said, "Only believe." The Bible says, "When He came to the house, [Jesus] did not allow anyone to enter with Him, except Peter and John and James, and the girl's father and mother" (Luke 8:51 NASB). By now, the father had taken a step of faith in trusting Jesus, and obviously his wife wanted to believe as well. The others that Jesus allowed to join Him inside the home were the members of His inner circle—the three disciples who also were present at the Transfiguration.

God truly works in mysterious ways, and He may not choose to work in the same way every time. Jesus restored this young girl completely to demonstrate His power over sin and death. There are times, however, when our son or daughter may not be healed. It is our responsibility to open the door of our hearts to Him and ask Him to come into our homes and the inner chambers of our thoughts and emotions where sorrow and fear linger. Only then can the Savior apply His healing balm of love and understanding as we allow Him to teach us how to deal with tribulation and adversity. We will not understand some of life's deepest disappointments until we walk hand in hand with Him in heaven. However, He always provides the insight we need.

Once while on a photography trip, darkness fell around me without much warning. I knew it was getting late, but I had no idea it would come so quickly. Because of the terrain, I knew I would have to hike back to base camp in darkness. I was grateful that I had packed flashlights in my daypack. A friend was with me and we quickly discovered these were only useful if we kept them pointed down on the path we were traveling. In other words, if we lifted them up and pointed them out in front of us, the light dissolved into the darkness. We could see a few feet farther, but suddenly the danger of tripping over exposed tree roots became a serious threat. This is when I thought of Psalm 119:105: "Your word is a lamp to my feet and a light to my path." There will be times when God only gives us enough light to take a few steps in front of us. We cannot see through the darkness clearly, and the temptation to become fearful over what could or could not happen is ever present. Jairus could have said, "Listen, my daughter is dead and all hope is gone. Plus, You have touched someone who is unclean. Coming to my house now would only bring more trouble and disappointment." But he didn't. Once he had decided to trust Jesus, he was determined to follow through on his commitment, and we need to do the same thing. When sickness or trauma comes to someone we love, especially one of our children, we may have to defy all human emotion and trust the One who provides the light of hope we need to get through each day.

When Suffering Does Not Make Sense

What we may view as deeply sorrowful, God views as an opportunity for His glory to be revealed. This was exactly what happened as Jesus restored Jairus's daughter. You may ask, "But what if God does not do the same for my daughter or son?" As painful as this answer is, you must come to a point where you are willing to allow Him to work in your life and the life of your child regardless of the outcome. He allows suffering for several reasons:

- Our faith is developed more in times of adversity than in times of blessing.
- We learn patience when we are forced to wait for God's answer or solution.
- If the pain continues long enough, our hearts are softened and we begin to desire Him above everything else this world holds as being dear.

God has a goal for our suffering. He uses it to draw us close to Himself. Over the years, I have experienced many trials—ones that I would never want to repeat. But I can say without hesitation that God has used each one to teach me something absolutely wonderful about His nature and especially His faithfulness. I did not enjoy hurting but the benefits that come as a result of difficulty and trial are priceless. In fact, if we truly want to learn the lessons God has for us, we must let go of our fear, desire for control, and feelings of frustration. The way we begin to do this is to ask Him to teach us how to bear the burden He has allowed.

"As time went on," the woman continued, "my husband and I began to pray with a greater depth. I don't know that this was marked by any single event. I do remember that suddenly I was aware that we were beginning to look up to God with open hands. We were not as interested in just plowing ahead. That was getting us nowhere. We were exhausted, and the doctors continued to be only interested in one thing and that was to treat our son's symptoms. While this was a good place for us to be, there were also dangers involved. The idea struck us that Satan may not want us to gain the victory. However, even though our lives were submitted to the Lord, we continued to search for a way to fix what was broken on our own. And the enemy enjoyed the fact that at this point, our faith was teetering. Could we trust God with everything, or did we need to help Him find a solution?"

We want life to make sense. We like order. Even people who feel out of control can seek to control their lives through their chaotic circumstances. While he may not have orchestrated the suffering we experience, he does seek to fill our minds with thoughts of fear, doubt, dread, and worry. If a child becomes sick, he takes great pleasure in us wondering if he is the cause of the illness. We can become so focused on what we think Satan is doing that we lose sight of what God wants to do in our lives. We need to be diligent in our walk with the Lord—not giving the enemy an opportunity to attack—but we also need to recall the truth: No power on earth or in heaven is greater than the God of the universe, and we are His children. The things that concern us concern Him to an even greater degree because He knows the purpose He has for our lives. Enduring great trials are often a part of His plan. The question He calls us to answer is this: Will we walk with Him through the valleys, trusting Him to bring us out on the other side?

CHAPTER 2

Maintaining a Right Focus

Usually when we find ourselves in serious trouble, we turn to the Psalms of David or the Epistles of Paul for help. It is in the writings of these men that we hear the echo of our own thoughts and questions: *What does God think about this situation? Does He care that my child is suffering? Why have these things happened? Maybe He doesn't really care that my family is hurting.* God cares, but He has a greater plan in mind for our suffering. As we watch our children struggle with illnesses and handicaps, we are constantly thinking about how they are suffering. The mental image tears at our hearts and threatens to immobilize us until we realize that many times our children are more trusting than we are. "Later, I asked my son, 'How did you deal with the fact that you were a teenager and could not do many of the activities that your friends were doing?'"

The woman, whose son's life had suddenly changed because of the seizures, wanted to know how he had come to grips with his illness. His answer was something she had not planned on hearing. "Mom, if this is it, then I'll learn to live with it." We can adapt to our suffering, but only if our lives are turned over to the Lord. Without Him—apart from His touch and intimate care—we will find ourselves fighting feelings of hopelessness and unimaginable sorrow. The one thing that will keep you centered and focused on the right things is a personal relationship with Jesus Christ. If you do not have this, then you will experience a level of hurt that goes beyond anything you can imagine. But when you understand that our loving God, who knows all about you, created you in love, and loves you with an eternal love, has a plan for your life regardless of your present circumstances, then you will find that there is hope even in a seemingly hopeless situation.

I remember how real this became to me after visiting the Roman prison where it is believed that the apostle Paul spent a great deal of time. You may wonder how his suffering relates to your own, especially when it involves a loved one that you cherish. All suffering, whether endured by an adult or a child, has to pass through the loving hands of an omnipotent God. Nothing escapes His notice. Paul was one of His most faithful servants, yet he suffered greatly. The condition of the prison where he was held was deplorable. It was nothing more than a hole dug in the ground. Prisoners were lowered into this chamber that often filled with water from a spring that flowed through an opening in the floor. Theologians have reported that there were also rodents present. We can only imagine the terrible conditions Paul had to endure. But here is the secret to his endurance: He was so wrapped up in God's care that regardless of his circumstances, he had a deep, abiding sense of contentment. Some of his greatest writings took place in the Mamertine Prison. And though he was a prisoner of Rome, he was incredibly free because the bonds that held him were earthly, not eternal. He knew one day he would shake off the chains that bound him and enter into the presence of God. Still, this was not his immediate goal because he knew to live, was to live as Christ.

I'll Be with You

God had a plan in mind for Paul's life, and He also has one for you and your family. Dealing with the highs and lows that accompany every trauma requires the right focus. Even though you may need help as you face emotions such as disappointment, anger, and grief, you can discover the peace that comes from trusting God. Learning this will not necessarily lead to a shortcut through suffering, but like the apostle Paul, you will learn that you are not alone. God is with you. When you read Paul's Prison Epistles—Ephesians, Philippians, and Colossians—you are reading the God-inspired words of a man who endured great difficulty to do what God had called him to do—preach the gospel to as many people as possible. Sometimes in order to remain effective, we have to shift our mind-set. Suffering comes and our lives take on a new dimension, a new message, and a new sense of ministry.

"In the beginning of my son's illness, one image stuck out in my mind," my friend said as she continued her story. "It was an image of being on a roller coaster. And I don't like the feeling that comes from being on these types of rides. I kept seeing this roller coaster running through my mind. This is exactly how my husband and I felt. It was as if we were on one long, continuous ride. One day while I was praying, I decided to tell the Lord just how I felt. 'I hate roller coasters,' I said with a strong resolve. Then suddenly, I sensed Him saying back to me, 'I know, but I am riding with you.' His presence and words took me so off guard that I remember ending my tirade of words and breaking down to cry. Suddenly, I knew He cared, and I knew that no matter what happened next, I could face it."

Coming to the realization that God cares about our hurts and personal struggles changes everything. This one fact has the ability to bring a sense of lightness to our burden. Though our circumstances may not change, our attitude can, and this is what changes us. Painful and narrow places in life have the ability to develop our character like nothing else. We will never find pleasure in knowing that our son or daughter is suffering or that someone we love is dealing with overwhelming circumstances. But we can find joy in the journey God has called us to travel if we learn how to rest in His presence, trusting Him for our deepest needs.

I remember receiving a telephone call one day that brought an inexplicable sense of sorrow to my life. It was horrendous news, and I could barely answer the caller. When I hung up the phone, only one thought raced through my mind: *Lord, if I truly believe what you have been teaching me all these years, then I have one choice and that is to trust You.* This is what I chose to do: trust Him and walk by faith, not by sight, every day. My circumstances were painful, but I can say without hesitation that God is faithful. He has never allowed me to experience anything beyond what He knows I can handle. But He also allows us to come to a point of desperation where we stop rushing and running around seeking answers to our problems apart from Him. He waits patiently until we exhaust every avenue and emotion and turn to Him for help.

You may think, *How can any of his words help me in my situation? Paul doesn't know what it feels like to watch someone battle for his or her life.* Yes, he does. He knows how to identify with our pain and sorrow. He experienced deep times of trial and also listened as others recounted the painful circumstances of their lives. Early Christians suffered heinous acts at the hands of the Roman emperors. Women and children faced persecution just as their fathers and husbands did. When you speak or write to someone about suffering and pain, you are speaking a universal language. Maybe your friends do not know what it feels like to live with a child who is battling a terminal illness or seizures or some other disease, but they can understand pain.

Paul writes,

For I want you to know how great a struggle I have on your behalf and for those who are at Laodicea, and for all those who have not personally seen my face, that their hearts may be encouraged, having been knit together in love, and attaining to all the wealth that comes from the full assurance of understanding, resulting in a true knowledge of God's mystery, that is, Christ Himself, in whom are hidden all the treasures of wisdom and knowledge. (Col. 2:1–3 NASB)

Earlier in chapter one he also wrote, "I rejoice in my sufferings for your sake" (1:24 NASB). How could Paul say, "I rejoice"? How can we even think of rejoicing when our lives feel as though they are being lived out on a roller coaster?

There is only one way, and Paul answered it while writing to the Philippian church. Remember, he was a prisoner—sometimes chained to a stone post—in a dark, lonely cell with no one to comfort him. "I want you to know, brethren, that my circumstances have turned out for the greater progress of the gospel, so that my imprisonment in the cause of Christ has become well known throughout the whole praetorian guard and to everyone else, and that most of the brethren, trusting in the Lord because of my imprisonment, have far more courage to speak the word of God without fear" (Phil. 1:12–14 NASB). What should this say to you and me about adversity? It says several things:

God is aware of our need. He instructs us to "cast your burden upon the LORD and He will sustain you; He will never allow the righteous to be shaken" (Ps. 55:22 NASB). When the bottom of life drops out, when the doctor steps into the room with heart-wrenching news, or when tragedy strikes without warning,

God will be beside us. He is committed to holding us up when the winds of adversity threaten to beat us down.

He uses adversity to draw us close to Himself. James reminds us to "draw near to God and He will draw near to you" (James 4:8 NASB). The principles of God do not change. Our circumstances can change instantly, but God does not change. The promises He gives us in His Word are true for every aspect of life. The challenge before you is an opportunity for Him to make His omnipotent presence known. But first, you must open your heart to Him. Perhaps through a simple prayer: "Lord, I need You. I'm so overwhelmed, and I don't know what way to turn. Please guide me. Give me the assurance I need that You are with me in this because I feel numb from the grief and pain I am experiencing." When you pray, God will answer.

He uses adversity to get our attention. At one of the lowest points in his life, David wrote, "The cords of death encompassed me, and the torrents of ungodliness terrified me. The cords of Sheol surrounded me; the snares of death confronted me. In my distress I called upon the LORD, and cried to my God for help; He heard my voice out of His temple, and my cry for help before Him came into His ears" (Ps. 18:4–6 NASB). God never planned for us to shoulder the weight of our burdens. He knows they are much too heavy for us to bear, especially alone. He uses each one as an effective tool in His hand to gain our attention. We can resist Him, but when we do, we miss a tremendous blessing. He has a plan for our sorrows. The question is, are we willing to trust Him enough to allow His plan to unfold in our lives?

In times of great trial, God expresses His love for us. This can be an extremely difficult truth to understand. But take a moment to listen to the words Paul wrote in 2 Corinthians 12: "There was given me a thorn in the flesh, a messenger of Satan to torment me—to keep me from exalting myself! Concerning this I implored the Lord three times that it might leave me. And He has said to me, 'My grace is sufficient for you, for power is perfected in weakness'" (vv. 7–9 NASB). The power Paul is talking about here is not personal strength. It is God's power. When God allows us to be placed in a narrow spot, He is not doing this to harm us. Instead, He uses the trial to draw us to Himself where we drop all our pretenses.

God uses heartache and suffering as catalysts to encourage us to examine our lives. The prophet Haggai wrote, "Consider your ways!" (Hag. 1:5 NASB). Luke recorded these words of Jesus: "Consider the lilies, how they grow: they neither toil nor spin; but I tell you, not even Solomon in all his glory clothed himself like one of these. But if God so clothes the grass in the field, which is alive today and tomorrow is thrown into the furnace, how much more will He clothe you?" (Luke 12:27, 28 NASB). More than likely, the issue before you is not one of clothing. If you have picked up this book, chances are someone close to you—a small child, a teenager, or a dear friend—is hurting and you feel at a loss to help. You have tried to have all the right answers, or perhaps, like the woman who is telling her story through this book, you are determined to find the answer to every problem. However, at this point you feel blocked—maybe by God, or maybe by your circumstances—and frustration and anger are filling your heart. God wants you to stop and examine your life and the situation before you. By examine, I don't mean to analyze it from a perspective of pain and hopelessness. I mean, stop and ask God to remove the blinders from your eyes so you can view this adversity from His perspective.

He is seeking to conquer any pride in our lives. Pride is an interesting subject because it can hide deep within our hearts. We can dress it up so it appears to be something totally acceptable. For example, we can appear to be humble and grateful, but deep inside we are thinking about what a good job we have done or how much our family has in comparison to others. God hates pride, and if there is a hint of this in our lives, He will expose it. Sometimes His methods seem harsh, but He only disciplines those He loves (Heb. 12:6). The author of Hebrews wrote, "It is for discipline that you endure; God deals with you as with sons; for what son is there whom his father does not discipline? . . . All discipline for the moment seems not to be joyful, but sorrowful; yet to those who have been trained by it, afterwards it yields the peaceful fruit of righteousness" (12:7, 11 NASB).

How can the sickness that your child is experiencing be used as discipline in your life? God is using your circumstances to train you concerning His ways. And He is shaping your life so you will become an instrument of love in your son or daughter's life. You are also in the process of learning how to comfort others who are facing similar devastating situations. You may want to shout, "But it is just not fair!" The Lord understands your frustration. While we do not know His mind fully concerning the death of His own Son, we can imagine a small portion of the grief He suffered as His Son—His beloved Son—hung dying on the cross. No human words were available to adequately express God's sorrow over the death of His Son. He had never been separated from the One He loved so purely and completely. Yet this is exactly what took place, and the pain and also the joy of the cross can only be fully recognized through a personal relationship with Jesus Christ. He died for us to know and experience the love of the Father each day no matter what befalls us. Pain trains us to set our focus on God—the one Person who loves us unconditionally and understands our deepest grief.

SUFFERING UNCOVERS OUR POTENTIAL

Over the years, I have often reminded the members of First Baptist Atlanta that God uses difficulty and trials to bring us to the end of ourselves so that we are totally dependent on Him. You may think there is a better way to accomplish this, but I can tell you from experience, adversity accomplishes this quicker than anything else. The woman whose son suddenly developed seizures admitted that the more she searched for a cure, the more she came to the realization that her son was more God's than he was hers. "I couldn't protect him. I tried. I did everything in my power to prevent him from ever suffering, but God had another plan." Though there was a time when she had thought her son's illness may have been primarily a spiritual issue, she became convinced that there was a physical cause to his problem, even if it had yet to be discovered. "The Lord gave me this truth, but He also gave me the promise that He would be with me.

"After a few months, I realized that this was not going to go away overnight. My husband and I would not suddenly wake up and discover that my son was well. What we did find is that over time we began to wake up thinking, *God, what do we do today? Should we keep searching for an answer or accept what we have been told?* Our prayers were changing, and though we did not know it at the time, we were changing too. There were times when I still felt like a failure. I doubted God. In fact, I doubted His ability and love for us. And I even felt guilty for feeling this way! Finally, a friend told me something I will never forget, 'God never said we would not get dirty fighting battles.'"

There are heartaches and disappointments God allows that we do not fully understand and we will get dirty at times fighting the good fight. But the longer we know Jesus, the more we will learn about His ways, and the more we will learn to trust Him in times of great emotional storm and anguish. What we usually discover is that the issue is not why God has allowed a sickness or event to happen as much as it is how we will respond to the trial and trouble. His goal is to teach us to turn to Him instead of others. He uses people in the medical profession in a tremendous way to diagnose our diseases, but far too often we look to them to be our saviors and have all the answers we need to our medical problems. There must be a balance where we seek God's wisdom and guidance along with the advice of the medical professionals He has given us.

"We went to every kind of doctor you could imagine," the woman said with a knowing smile. "I believe God knew we would have to keep running until we ran out of doctors and energy. But I don't know if I ever did, and this is the one thing that I look back on and wish I could change by taking more time to pray and allow Him to lead us. God allowed us to discover the right doctor through a crazy turn of events. Once while I was in the dentist's office, I mentioned my son's situation. He knew of another dentist in Florida, whom he thought could help. We immediately made an appointment. After hearing our story, this new dentist asked us to make an appointment with a neurologist he knew at a teaching hospital connected with a university in Florida.

"At first we were hesitant, but we also wondered if God was leading us along this route. By this time, we had slowed down enough to consider what He may want us to do or not do. We had seen neurologists in the past and the answer was always the same: 'There is no hope, and you need to accept the truth.' This time, the situation proved to be different. The neurologist had an MRI machine, and we were about to begin to discover the truth. Yet the full answer was a year away. Our odyssey was about to take an entirely different turn. And the one thing we realized was this: even in our stumbling attempt to play God, the Lord never abandoned His love for us. He was totally in control of us, the doctors, and the timing of my son's healing."

One of the ways we advance through adversity is by coming to a point where we no longer want a quick fix to our problems. Instead, we want to learn what God has for us beginning with understanding the reality of His sovereignty. When we acknowledge that God is sovereign, we also acknowledge that regardless of the outcome, He knows what is best for our lives. We can thank Him for our infirmities, weaknesses, adversities, hardships, trials, tribulations, setbacks, disappointments, and disillusionments because we know that these play a specific role in His eternal plan. But as long as we think we can solve our own problems, God will allow us to go through life's difficulties feeling alone. We usually do not get very far before we realize the tragedy that accompanies this type of spiritual loneliness.

The moment we admit our weakness and need for Him, God begins to move on our behalf by opening doors of hope. This may include physical healing, or it may mean giving us the courage and support we need to keep going forward. The psalmist wrote: "The angel of the LORD encamps around those who fear Him, and rescues them. . . . The righteous cry, and the LORD hears and delivers them out of all their troubles. The LORD is near to the brokenhearted and saves those who are crushed in spirit. Many are the afflictions of the righteous, but the LORD delivers him out of them all" (34:7, 17–19 NASB).

If we never faced persecution, opposition, or tribulation, we would miss one of the most awesome things about God—His extreme care and love for us. We would miss His fellowship and the extreme care that He provides in times of crisis. I have talked with people, who have never really allowed themselves to feel the full impact of God's loving arms surrounding them. They always are on guard, ready to protect their hearts from being hurt, and refusing to allow Him to work in and through adversity. If adversity strikes, they try to come up with a solution, a plan, and a reason for the distress.

Pain hurts. Seeing a loved one suffer is anything but easy. Feeling helpless leaves us struggling to find even an ounce of hope. We want to give up, and in a way, God is waiting for us to do just that, but not give up the way the world does. He wants us to throw our arms up and hold them there so He can lift us up and embrace us with His love. Don't be afraid to tell Him that you are hurting, fearful, and needy. He knows this. And please do not be afraid to allow Him to counsel and care for you. He is God, but He is also our truest Friend. It is in the center of a storm that we learn to cling to Him. We may learn to like Him in times of happiness, but if you truly want to see God's power in operation and learn how to really love Him, open your heart to Him when trouble strikes and you feel helpless.

Paul said, "I count all things to be loss in view of the surpassing value of knowing Christ Jesus my Lord, for whom I have suffered the loss of all things" (Phil. 3:8 NASB). He wrote "all things to be loss" after he had given a long explanation of his own heritage. In Philippians he wrote, "If anyone else has a mind to put confidence in the flesh, I far more: circumcised the eighth day, of the nation of Israel, of the tribe of Benjamin, a Hebrew of Hebrews; as to the Law, a Pharisee; as to zeal, a persecutor of the church; as to the righteousness which is in the Law, found blameless. But whatever things were gain to me, those things I have counted as loss for the sake of Christ" (3:5–7). In other words, nothing—not even the honor, education, and tradition of this world is more valuable than knowing Christ. How do you come to a place where you want to know God? How do you know what He is really like? You will never know God until you come to a point where you understand that this includes walking through adversity with Him.

When our children hurt, we hurt too. When we hear them cry, we also want to cry. God does the same thing. He sees us hurting, and like a loving Father, He wants to prevent the misery that is bringing such pain to our lives, but He knows that suffering is a natural part of our world. Therefore, He allows it and uses it to refocus our attention to a point where we see Him through the trial, the heartache, and the disappointment.

Adversity is one of God's choicest tools. But in His loving omnipotent hand, difficulty and heartache become catalysts for the greatest lessons we can learn—lessons that teach us that He is trustworthy, faithful, true, long-suffering, and gentle. You may have to reach a point where you say, "God, it is all over. I can smell defeat, death, and disappointment, but I know You are faithful because You are God!" When we can say this, we will sense His hand of mercy wrapping around our hearts and lives. Our focus will be set on Him and Him alone. Then the journey—the burden that once seemed so heavy—will be light! (Matt. 11:30).

CHAPTER 3

Moving Beyond Your Feelings

Feelings of fear, guilt, anger, and frustration usually mean we are focusing on ourselves. It is perfectly normal to run through an index of emotions while dealing with a child's pain and suffering. One father told me, "I feel so guilty because it is not me who is hurting. If I could take the place of my daughter, I would gladly do it." While guilt is a common response, it also has the ability to change our focus. If we become fixated on our feelings, then we will not be able to comfort our children when they need us the most. It is understandable to feel remorse, guilt, and even fear of the unknown. But, especially as Christians, we must find a way to get our eyes off ourselves and onto God. After all, He is the source of our strength and hope.

When a child is fighting for his life, he needs his mom and dad to be fully tuned into God's will and ways. Otherwise bitterness and anger could grow and prevent us from learning what God wants to teach. We may wonder, *Why would God allow such suffering?* In times of trial, we quickly learn that there is not a simple answer to this question. The enemy will try to trick us into saying words like *if only* or *should*. For example, "I should have taken him to the doctor sooner." "If only I had thought about taking a different route home, we would have avoided the accident."

GIVE YOUR REGRETS TO GOD

I remember my mother saying to me, "I always regretted the fact that when you were young I could not give you the things other parents gave their children." She had carried a deep sense of guilt for a long time. Growing up in a single parent home was difficult. I never knew my father because he died when I was seven months old. Mother worked two jobs just to keep food on our table. Because of this, I may have missed some of the things other children enjoyed. We moved several times, and nothing is more unsettling to a young child than having to change schools and friends repeatedly. Still, I can honestly say that I did not have a great sense of loss or that I was missing out on something. Instead, I felt as though I had been given a great gift. My mom loved me and was committed to taking care of me the best she could.

I told her, "Mom, you have nothing to regret. You gave me something money could not buy. It cannot be manufactured or purchased. You planted a love for God in my heart. You taught me how to pray, to obey Him, and to do His will. You also demonstrated to me a life of faith. We were totally dependent on Him." I would rather have the memory of her love and devotion to God and to me than anything else. When children are young, they do not care about what they have or do not have. We are the ones who draw lines of distinction by insisting that they have the latest and greatest of everything. By the time they are walking, they are demanding things that most of us never considered owning when we were young.

I have seen families endure great suffering, but it is not because God's love for them has faded. Sometimes suffering comes as a result of the fallen nature of our world. Other times it comes because a person has turned away from God's love and become involved in sin. The cold hard truth about Satan's persistence is that he wants to destroy the family. He also wants to trip us and discourage us to prevent us from becoming the people God created us to be. Therefore, he will stop at nothing to derail our devotion to the Lord. One of the most devastating and tangible evidences of his wickedness is the attack he launches against our families. We must realize that we are on Satan's radar screen. Temptation and lust are just two of the weapons he uses to lure men and women into deadly sin. And, sadly, the people who end up being hurt the most are our children. Parents can become so focused on their individual needs being met that they never take time to stop and consider what their actions are doing to their children.

THE TRUTH ABOUT GUILT

Years ago a man who was a member of my church made an appointment with me. I assumed that since he and his wife were new church members, he wanted to talk to me about how they could become more involved. I quickly found out differently. He sat down and looked straight into my eyes and asked, "Dr. Stanley, how much time did you spend with your son last week?" Andy was only twelve years old and had no connection with this man or his children. In fact, no one in my family knew them. He went on to explain how he believed that God was prompting him to encourage me to spend more time with my children. I thought about his question for the rest of the day and ended up going home early that evening.

Andy had been asking me to take him fishing in a small pond that was owned by one of our neighbors. We had gone fishing there a couple of times and had a really good time. On that day I was guilt-stricken and could not recall how long it had been since we had time together doing this sort of thing. I realized Andy needed me and I also needed him. Since my father had died before I even knew him, I had never had a good role model for a father. My stepfather was abusive and did not come to know the Lord until much later in life. Therefore, anything I learned was the result of my own relationship with God. He is our heavenly Father, and He knows exactly how to deal with our emotions.

God had to make me aware of my shortcomings. I wanted my children to grow up knowing how much I loved them. I could have stopped trying and said, "I don't know how to be a good Dad because I did not have a good role model." Instead, I chose to learn as much as I possibly could. I also had to learn to listen to what my children were saying. If they felt I was not home enough, then I wanted to know this. We should never miss the opportunities God has given us to be a part of our children's lives. I cannot say that I learned the lesson perfectly. I failed at times, just like every parent, but I can say that over the years I have only wanted to grow deeper and richer in this area. Today one of the greatest joys I have is being with my grandchildren.

Feelings of guilt can stir up a host of other emotions—fear of punishment, thoughts of isolation, and a sense of rejection, along with feelings of depression, worthlessness, and shame. In times of adversity, when our thinking is not very clear, we can confuse these feelings with what is true. God always has a goal in mind for true guilt. These feelings can also be used by God to get our attention. If we have disobeyed Him, He may allow us to feel guilt to get the right response from us. However, if the feelings we have are free floating—in other words, there is no reason, no known sin, or deliberate wrong behavior—then what we may be feeling is false guilt, which is not from God but from Satan.

How do you discern true guilt from false guilt?

True guilt is convicting. We sin and immediately sense the Holy Spirit telling us that what we have done is wrong. Over the years, I have watched people deal with feelings of guilt. Some have even walked up to me at church wanting to confess their sin. While I do listen, especially if they have come forward at the end of a service, I point them to God and His unconditional forgiveness. To experience God's cleansing, they must turn to Him in prayer and confess their sin. Then they must be willing to turn away from sin and accept His mercy and forgiveness. If sin has devastated their lives or the lives of those in their family, this can be hard to do. Usually the person or persons will try to find a way to continue carrying feelings of guilt around with them. Jesus said, "If the Son makes you free, you will be free indeed" (John 8:36 NASB). This does not mean that the consequences of sin will not remain. But it does mean that we can be forgiven and watch as God restores our fellowship with Him.

True guilt directs us to God. Guilt that is from God always has a goal, which is to bring us back to God. We drift in our devotion to Him, and suddenly our world appears dark and stormy. Adversity strikes, and we realize that instead of being in the center of His care, we are lingering along the outskirts of devotion where feelings of complacency and compromise live. The danger we face is this: when we chose not to deal with guilt by admitting we have acted wrongly and unwisely before God, then it will deal with us.

I was recently talking with a good friend who is a Christian psychologist, and he confirmed that many of the physical problems we face today are the result of feeling guilty. This is true even among people who are not Christians. Guilt is not an evangelical issue. Even children know when they have acted in a way that is wrong. It washes over their faces. This is because God created us with an inner compass to help us discern right from wrong. However, the lines between these two become increasingly more blurred with the decline of godly moral values. At one time it was not acceptable for a young person to engage in sexual contact before marriage. Today, however, by the world's standards, it is quite acceptable and even considered normal, but not by God's. The hurt many young people experience comes as a direct result of sin. And when we sin, we are going to feel guilty. But there is a Someone who loves us unconditionally and that is Jesus Christ. He is the only Person who can forgive and take away the guilt and punishment of sin.

True guilt is useful. Nothing is more valuable in the life of a believer than godly confession and remorse. And nothing brings us to a point of admitting that we have done something wrong faster than a sense of guilt. We often use the phrase, "I feel guilty." But this is not always a bad thing. Guilt can be God's tool of choice in the lives of many who have chosen not to obey Him. The author of Hebrews reminds us that we have a high priest who hears our confessions and forgives our sins (5:5, 6). There is only one basis upon which God forgives sin and that is the fact that His Son, the Lord Jesus Christ, died at Calvary, shed His blood, and paid your sin debt in full. On that basis, and that basis alone, sin is forgiven. And only when you accept Jesus as your Savior by faith in confession and repentance of your sin can you claim the forgiveness of God.

The person who is an unbeliever will feel guilty. His feelings are legitimate because the reality is this: he or she is guilty. The only solution to this problem is the grace of God, which is provided through the shed blood of Jesus Christ. Sin demands atonement. And Christ's death paid the penalty for our sin. This truth is foundational to every aspect of the Christian life. You cannot fully trust God until you realize that He not only has given you the opportunity to experience eternal life, but He is also trustworthy and faithful. He promised that the grave would not hold Him and it did not. Therefore, sin and death have no power over Him. The apostle Paul wrote, "God, being rich in mercy, because of His great love with which He loved us, even when we were dead in our transgressions, made us alive together with Christ (by grace you have been saved)" (Eph. 2:4, 5 NASB). The moment we seek His forgiveness through prayer, God turns in our direction. God does not want us to languish in the shadows of guilt.

False guilt is counterproductive. This is probably the one thing that prevents people from really understanding the process that accompanies adversity. Trouble strikes and they immediately assume it is the result of something they have done. This may not be the case. We mentioned earlier that sins such as adultery have serious and far-reaching consequences. I always tell my congregation that we reap what we sow, more than we sow, and later than we sow it. That is the legacy of sin. However, false guilt is an entirely different emotion where a person feels shameful for something he or she did not do. While godly guilt has a focused set of goals—confession, repentance, and restoration—false guilt is not centralized on any one incident. You find yourself feeling guilty for no apparent reason. Worse is the fact that you begin to view yourself as being worthless and someone others would not enjoy knowing.

False guilt has the opposite effect of godly remorse. It condemns and convicts without leading a person to embrace God's love, forgiveness, and acceptance. Without these, we cannot sense His close presence in times of need. When our hearts are hurting, He wants to rush to our aid. But if our only view of God is a condemning judge, then we will not experience the freedom He wants us to have. I'm not talking about being free from sorrow, though I do believe that people who go through terminal illnesses with children can and do come to a point where there is a joy within their hearts that we cannot know or understand. They have found a secret place of shelter and hope within the confines of God's loving care. Feelings of false guilt will not take you to this place. There is only one way and that is through an intimate relationship with Jesus Christ. Nothing else has the ability to bring a lasting sense of calm and hopeful perspective to our hearts and lives.

False guilt is spiritually debilitating. It drains away our hope and leaves us wondering why God would inflict such pain. Did we really do something so heinous that there is no relief for us or those we love? Once again, when you have this type of view, your thinking is locked on one thing: yourself. Instead of telling God exactly how you feel, you immediately assume that He is judging your life and you are liable for something that you really have no control over. He never seeks to punish us. He may allow circumstances or consequences as a result of poor choices we make, but He never purposefully harms anyone.

False guilt is self-centered. There are times when we need to confess the way we feel. My mother found a way to tell me about her own struggle with guilt. Always remember, the one thing that defuses guilt is truth. God's truth given to us through His Word annihilates false guilt. Likewise, I was able to tell Mom the truth concerning my childhood. I'm where I am today as a result of the discipline I received in those early years. You may think, *But you suffered. You had to get up in the morning and cook your own breakfast and get ready and go to school. Then when you came home, you had to study and eat dinner alone. That had to be difficult to bear.* I have never thought about my circumstances from that perspective. While I would not advocate leaving a five-year-old child at home alone in today's world, I can say without a doubt that God was watching over me. He knew that there would be a time when I would have the opportunity to identify with someone else, who felt lonely as a child or had to do something difficult that they did not enjoy. Life's sorrows and challenges always provide opportunities for us to grow and mature—not just physically, but spiritually, emotionally, and mentally. But false guilt prevents this from taking place.

"I really think I missed what God was wanting to teach me," the woman whose son was having seizures said. "I couldn't protect him and could not find healing for him. So I felt guilty and helpless. I don't think I ever got past this fact until after the Lord healed him. Then I remember thinking, *The one thing God wants me to do is to trust Him.* He wanted me to trust Him with my son, my emotions, and misconceived ideas. He wanted me to stop feeling guilty or like I needed to have all the answers. In other words, He wanted me to rest in His care, and this is the hardest thing to do, especially when you see your child suffering."

LIVING BEYOND GUILT

How do we correctly handle feelings of guilt and regret? (Rom. 8:1)

Realize God loves you and He loves your child. This is the most important first step we must take. Once we gain insight into God's ways, we look at life from a different perspective. It all begins by opening ourselves up to the fact that God loves us. When a child grows up in a home where he does not feel loved, he will have an overriding sense of guilt because he will think, *I must have done something wrong or things would be different.* The atmosphere within the home may be tense because his parents have never understood or accepted the unconditional love of God. They have spent their entire lives working to gain a certain social image or to maintain a degree of control over their lives. In an atmosphere like this, a child can feel restricted and become tempted to think, *If only I would try harder, maybe Mom would see that I'm doing the best I can do.*

When a pastor or Christian counselor suggests turning to God in prayer, a person may ignore the advice because he does not believe he can trust anyone but himself. Nothing could be further from the truth! The only Person we can trust to love us at all times is God. He understands us and He loves us even when we sin and refuse to admit our failures. His love is not based on our performance; it is based on Christ's obedience at Calvary. Seeking His forgiveness is the way we become free from the bondages of guilt, shame, and most of all, sin. God never stops loving us, which is the very reason we need Him. His love changes us so that we live our lives for Him and also learn how to comfort others who are hurting.

Remember, God's ways are not your ways. Many times our first reaction to bad news is to feel hurt and wonder why this event or sickness happened to someone we love so much. How can you explain the terminal illness of a child who is innocent or the abuse of a young person? We cannot. Only God has the answers, and many times He may not tell us the complete reason why He has allowed the adversity. This is where faith and trust must take hold. When it comes to guilt, a major problem is our understanding and concept of who God is. Usually it is one of personal guilt because we view ourselves as not living up to God's or our expectations. And because we have failed so many times, we feel as though He could not possibly help or love us. This line of thinking is totally wrong.

Remember the question that the disciples asked before Jesus healed the man born blind? "'Rabbi, who sinned, this man or his parents, that he would be born blind?' Jesus answered, 'It was neither that this man sinned, nor his parents; but it was so that the works of God might be displayed in him'" (John 9:2, 3

NASB). God allowed this man to suffer many years for His glory to be displayed. We rarely consider this line of thinking when we are in the midst of adversity, especially when the trial is intense and continues for a long period of time. However, it is the very point that God wants us to understand. When we focus on Him instead of on our circumstances, He is glorified and we are strengthened so we can endure the painful journey we have been called to travel.

Place your Trust in Christ. When we begin to gain the right perspective, we will better understand God's work in our lives. "I had to come to a point where I was willing to trust God regardless of whether my son was healed or not. When my husband and I came to the end of ourselves, we found that we were right where we needed to be—on our faces before God in His presence. He was not going to give up; we were the ones who needed to learn to trust Him. He knew where my son's suffering was taking us, and it was not where we thought we needed to go. We wanted him to be healed immediately so we could go on with life. God, however, had other plans."

Children can hurt in many different ways. Some may have horrendous diseases that end in death. Others can hurt as the result of drug abuse, alcoholism, abuse, or emotional problems. There are a number of reasons for adversity. But the questions we must answer are: How do we as parents move past our own feelings of anger, insecurity, guilt, and resentment toward God? Can we surrender our children to Him—not abandoning them in times of darkness, but allowing Him to work in their lives?

There are no easy answers to the questions that arise within our hearts when we are faced with sickness, disease, and heartache. However, we have a Savior who suffered greatly, personally knows the weight of every temptation we face, and knows exactly how to comfort us in times of great trial and remorse. How do you move past feelings of guilt? You must acknowledge your feelings to God. When you involve Him in the problem you are facing, the weight of your burden quickly diminishes because you are no longer struggling alone. He is in the battle with you. Sometimes it may be difficult to identify exactly what caused the emotion you are feeling. This has been true for me. However, I can say that it has been a wonderful, exciting, and sometimes painful journey as I have watched God pull back the covers of my life and peel off the skin of the years to show me the things that I did not know about myself. He has brought a wonderful sense of freedom to my life. Pain purifies us. It all boils down to this: I either have to choose to believe what He said about me and live free or follow my feelings and suffer in an even greater way.

CHAPTER 4

When the Answer Doesn't Come

What is God doing when He remains silent and makes us wait without an answer or a solution to our problem for a long period of time? How do we handle the seemingly hopeless times when we want Him to intervene in our daughter or son's life, but He doesn't? We know they are suffering, but instead of the hurt easing, it seems to become more intense. How can we stand by and watch and wait? God always has an answer to our unmet need.

Jesus met a woman while traveling throughout the cities of Tyre and Sidon who was desperate for a solution to her horrendous situation. Her daughter was possessed by a demon, and more than likely, she had exhausted all human avenues of hope seeking help for her daughter. Matthew wrote that she was "a

Canaanite woman from that region" (15:22, 23 NASB). He wanted us to have even greater insight into this woman's life and need. The fact that he tells us she was a Canaanite—the very people who at one time were Israel's dire enemies—is significant. We can surmise there was a sense of unworthiness attached to her life. She knew the Jews viewed her and her family as being unclean and pagan. This reveals how she felt about being in the Savior's presence. But it also helps us understand the reaction of Christ's followers.

However, when you are desperate for an answer or a cure, you will do almost anything. Human pride and an attitude of self-righteousness quickly fade. While the Lord did not view her as an enemy of old, He did see her as being a Gentile and someone who had not been given the same rights and privileges as the Jews. At this point, He had come to earth as the Messiah to the Jews and, later, to the Gentiles. Still, He was God, and He felt compassion for this woman. Matthew continued, "A Canaanite woman from that region came out and began to cry out, saying, 'Have mercy on me, Lord, Son of David; my daughter is cruelly demon-possessed.' But He did not answer her a word. And His disciples came and implored Him, saying 'Send her away, because she keeps shouting at us'" (Matt. 15:22, 23 NASB). The disciples were probably frustrated because this woman would not leave them alone. She was very determined—enough so to gain a mention in Matthew's gospel and for good reason. While the disciples believed Jesus' mission was strictly to the Jewish people, God was poised to answer her prayers, but first there was silence and a time of waiting.

HOW LONG, LORD?

Have you ever thought about how long some men and women in the Bible had to wait to see God intervene in their situation? Everyone who received healing had to wait. Some suffered most of their lives, others for a relatively short period of time, but because the emotional and physical pain was so intense, it surely felt much longer. Moses waited forty years before God led him back to Egypt, where he became a deliverer to the nation of Israel. David waited for years to ascend to Israel's throne. Though he was anointed king when he was quite young, his coronation did not take place for a very long time. The man born blind waited most of his life to be healed. More than likely, he had given up hope. Then he heard about Jesus. When he heard the Savior was walking in his direction, he shouted out to Him and asked for mercy (Mark 10:47).

Maybe you feel as if you can wait no longer. The storm winds have torn holes in your life. You have watched as your child has gone from one bad situation to another. You have prayed, believing God was listening, but He has not answered your prayers. You have sought out all the verses in His Word that could be connected to your situation and even a few more. You have prayed each one back to the Lord and listened for His response, but He is quiet—silent and still. Is He sleeping? Does He care? The answer is yes. He has not abandoned you. He is not being cruel or unloving. He is near, and while you feel as though you cannot continue listening to another doctor's report, you can because He will give you the strength you need.

Even though we may not see the physical evidence of God's work, His is on the move. The psalmist wrote, "[God] will not allow your foot to slip; He who keeps you will not slumber. . . . The LORD is your keeper; The LORD is your shade on your right hand. The sun will not smite you by day, nor the moon by night. The LORD will protect you from all evil; He will keep your soul. The LORD will guard your going out and your coming in from this time forth and forever" (121:3, 5–8 NASB). A storm is nothing more than evidence of His mighty presence. If we are to survive life's tempests, we must change the way we view them. So often I have a young man or woman tell me, "I can't make it. I feel so discouraged." What this person is saying is: "I'm afraid! I did not know life was going to turn out this way. I had a plan and I believed it was God's plan too. Now everything is a mess."

One college student confided that he did not think he could marry the girl he had known and loved for several years. I asked him why he felt this way and he said, "I watched my mom and dad go through a terrible divorce. I just don't think I could put our children through that same thing." He wasn't even married and the subject of children had not been discussed, but he was sure that he would fall flat on his face in the area of marriage simply because his mother and father's marriage ended. Just because others go through a certain trial does not mean this will be repeated in our lives. In some cases, children can feel blame or responsibility that can impact them as adults. Therefore, we need to be sensitive to their feelings. Even if they are much older, when something like divorce comes, we need to assure them of our love and care. Also, we must remind them that they did not contribute in any way to the problem. Younger children especially can be affected by the separation of their parents. They may not be as quick to say, "I am hurting and I feel as though you are mad at me. I think I did something to cause all of this." Yet these feelings are common, and they are innocent bystanders who have been gathered up in the vortex of pain and suffering.

One of the first things we need to do when we sense our children hurting is to stop and consider how we are handling the situation. I assured the young man who had come to me for counseling that he could, with God's help, get married and stay married. He did not need to avoid taking this step in life simply because he had witnessed the crumbling of his parent's relationship. There are many aspects of God's nature that bring hope and encouragement, but one that I find the most comforting is the fact that He is sovereign. He never changes. There is nothing we can do to shift His faithfulness. We may not understand why He has allowed a certain form of suffering to touch our lives, but we can be sure of one thing: He will carry us through the difficulty. And we do not have to be fearful to step out and trust Him for healing and wholeness in any area.

Are we being appropriately honest with them? Sometimes our children are not mature enough to handle all of the truth. One mother told me, "I have told my daughter [who was about ten years old at the time] the entire story. She knows it all!" I cringed at her words because I knew this child was too young to handle the details of her parent's separation. The burden was too great for her to bear, not to mention the fact that her maturation level was not developed enough for her to handle the complicated issues surrounding a problem like this. The same is true when it comes to serious illness. Truth can be told in a way that a child can assimilate it. Of course, when another sibling is dying or a mom and dad are on their way to a divorce, any truth is painful, but it must be told. I'm just convinced that asking God to give us the right wording at the right time is essential for communication lines to remain open so our children will feel safe to express any feelings of guilt or anger.

An older child may need to take some time to be alone and think through what he has heard. You must give him space but continue to reaffirm your love for him on a consistent basis. I have seen parents go through separations never thinking about the emotional pain their children were suffering until after all the divorce papers were signed. They were too caught up in their own feelings—what they would do next, how they would continue, did God still love them? As they worked through these questions, they failed to consider that their children needed to know that their lives count and they are deeply loved.

Are we listening to what they are saying as well as what they are not saying? Children may or may not tell us what they are thinking. A friend of mine who is a Christian psychologist assures me that what I have read is right: Most of our communication takes place on a nonverbal level. From the time we are born until we breathe our last breath, we are communicating something to someone. You may say, "I rarely say anything unless I'm asked a question." That may be true, but you are still communicating something with your body posture, the way you walk, hold your shoulders, smile, wrinkle your brow, or any number of things. We send off thousands of nonverbal cues to the people we come in contact with even on a limited basis. We can let them know that we are happy, tired, frustrated, or filled with sorrow through our voice inflection or by the way we hold our heads.

In a normal environment such as a neighborhood meeting or lunch at the office, others may not think to ask, "How are you doing?" and then hang around to hear the answer. We can come across as being very uncaring when we ask with our voices, "How has your day been?" but our body language says, "I'm out of here. I have to go and do something else." If we are going to be caring people that reflect the love of Christ to a hurting world, we must be willing to enter the battle with our hearts and always on our knees.

I tell parents to "listen" to what is *not* being said as much as what is being voiced. A drop in grades at school is a sure sign that your child needs your attention, but there are other signs too. Anything that seems out of place or not in keeping with your son or daughter's consistent behavior should be addressed or watched. Some parents have expressed that they do not want to invade their child's privacy, but healthy invasion can be a saving factor if that child is withdrawing. We can be sure that any sudden withdrawal can lead to negative results. Children do not have to be social butterflies, but they should be able to communicate honestly with friends, teachers at church and school, and most of all, with parents who love them.

If you are unsure how to talk with your child about a certain problem or issue, a trusted Christian counselor or pastor may offer the help you need. You also can learn how to ask solid leading questions such as "When your brother or sister is hurting, how does that make you feel?" and "When Daddy (or Mommy) is not home, what do you think about this?"

Children's hospitals have wonderful programs to teach us how to cope and deal with consequences of a long-term illness. However, the parents' job is to remind their children that God is still in control regardless of what happens. He is their shelter and He understands everything they are feeling because at some point He had felt the same way. "For since He Himself was tempted in that which He has suffered, He is able to come to the aid of those who are tempted" (Heb. 2:18 NASB).

Are we willing to ask God to show us how to lay aside our selfish feelings to help our children cope with the pain and the difficulty that comes from a long-term illness or problem? Dealing with the stress of adversity can be very demanding. Many of us have sat at the bedside of loved ones in the hospital. Hour after hour, we have held their hand and assured them that we are near. Yet over time, we can become very focused on our needs and plans. Emotionally, when trouble comes, we must shift from a position of independence to one of total dependence on God. As long as we insist on "saving" our family from all trouble and pain, we will be weighed down by the burden and grow weary quickly.

If we only look at ourselves—how the problem affects us— we will miss the tremendous blessing that God has for us. Not only that, we will miss the experience that comes from walking hand in hand with Him through the valley. Ask yourself, "Am I willing to lay enough of 'me' aside so that God can reveal Himself to me and to others through my life?" Or is it your goal to walk quickly through the problem and "just get by" so it will be over? If that is the case, then I'm afraid you will find yourself repeating the lesson over and over again until you have learned what the Lord has for you to learn. If you look at a map of the route Israel took in the wilderness, you would probably say, "My goodness, they traveled in a huge circle!" And I would have to agree.

They resisted God on several occasions, and He just kept applying the pressure until they were willing to be the people He created them to be. The same is true for us. God has a plan for the adversity we face. Could He accomplish His will another way? Only He knows for sure. However, the one thing we can admit without hesitation is that when trouble strikes, one of the first things we say is, "God, why?" He wants that "why" to be followed by, "Lord, even though I do not under-stand why this has happened, I want You to know that I love

You and I am willing to go through the valley, if this is where You want me to travel."

I often meet people who feel overwhelmed by their circumstances. They cannot think clearly about God's care for them because fear has so gripped their heart that they cannot move forward in their thinking. They are fixated on the wrong thing and in doing so they deny God's sovereignty and omnipotent strength. Nothing is greater than God—no disease, addiction, or fear. He is above and over all things. And He has promised never to leave us. When we are so exhausted and to a point where we feel as though we cannot take another step, He reminds us that He will bear our burdens for us, if we will allow Him to do this (Ps. 55:22).

Matthew moves quickly and picks up the story of the Canaanite woman as he writes, "[Jesus] answered and said, 'I was sent only to the lost sheep of the house of Israel.' But she came and began to bow down before Him, saying, 'Lord, help me!'" (15:24, 25 NASB). This woman cried out for help as only a mother of a hurting child can do. She was not going to take no for an answer, and she demonstrated a level of faith that many people fail to do. Even though she did not know Jesus, she believed in His ability and bowed down before Him. In doing so, she gained the Savior's attention. He held firm: "'It is not good to take the children's bread and throw it to the dogs.' But she said, 'Yes, Lord; but even the dogs feed on the crumbs which fall from their masters' table'" (vv. 26, 27 NASB).

Imagine for a moment how this woman felt. Perhaps, she

had heard about Jesus—who He was and His ability to heal. She had no hope to offer her daughter. The misery and sorrow this woman felt was great. She knew the problem was far beyond her ability to handle. But it was not beyond Christ's ability. Therefore, she refused to allow human barriers such as race and false assumptions to prevent her from reaching her goal, which was to see her daughter healed and restored. She was even willing to debate the Lord and in her conquest ended up demonstrating great faith. There are times when God will call on us to endure hardship beyond a point that we think is necessary or effective. He is the one who knows what He wants to accomplish in our lives.

"Then Jesus said to her, 'O woman, your faith is great; it shall be done for you as you wish.' And her daughter was healed at once" (Matt. 15:28 NASB). Jesus had compassion for this Gentile woman, whose faith had moved Him to the point of action. There are times when God does physically heal those who have a terminal illness or injury. Other times He may not choose to heal this way. Regardless, He wants us to be free of anxiety, fear, dread, and worry. Even when the inevitable comes, we do not face it alone. He is with us, and He has a purpose for every tragedy, trial, and heartache. In some cases, He may give us insight into why these things have happened. Other times, He simply calls us to trust Him even though our circumstances do not make sense. "By faith . . . [Moses] endured, as seeing Him who is unseen" (Heb. 11:27 NASB). In many cases, we may have to do the same thing—endure. This usually includes waiting for a longer period of time than we think is necessary. But from God's perspective it is exactly what is needed. Waiting teaches us a level of patience and endurance that we cannot learn any other way. The pace of our world is hurried. We want instant results. I was listening to an ad on the radio recently for a printing firm and their key marketing pitch was the "quickest turnaround time in the industry." No one wants to wait, but so often this is exactly what God wants us to do because He knows that we will learn much more in the heat of affliction than in the calmness of comfort and pleasure.

THE STORY CONTINUES

"I came to realize it was through the time spent in waiting for God to work that I came to know Him in a far greater way," my friend insisted. "I believed there was a physical reason for his seizures, and I became solely convinced that finding the answer would not be something that happened overnight. As I read the story of the woman who pleaded with Jesus to heal her daughter, I found myself thinking, *Okay, God, it is You and me and my husband and no one else. No matter how long it takes, we're not going to give up.* When the answer came, we could hardly believe it.

"The doctors at the new hospital where we had been advised to go ordered an MRI, which is a normal part of diagnosis today, but in the late '80s this procedure was not as common as it is today. Had it been, doctors would have found the small, marble-size, non-cancerous cyst that had formed on my son's brain. This was believed to be the cause of his seizures. However, what we also discovered was that the doctors were not eager to operate. It was a dangerous procedure. Therefore, they suggested that we wait another year and during this time try a new seizure medication. My heart sank because I did not think I could bare the thought of him having another episode.

"It also was so hard to watch the effects the drugs had on his life. They caused him to become lethargic, which meant it was extremely difficult for him to focus on the work he had to do for his college classes. There also was the danger that they could cause permanent liver damage. Therefore, we had to submit to regular blood tests in order to monitor the health of his liver. Even the radiologist who performed our tests confirmed that he felt the problem was the cyst but conceded, 'We need to do what they are asking.' We had waited so long and now we had to wait even longer."

How Can I Keep Going?

Sometimes, God breaks into the storm that has besieged our lives and other times He allows us to ride it out. Jesus walked on the water to the disciples who were bouncing around furiously in their wind-swept boat. Even though they were seasoned fishermen, they were convinced they were about to perish! How many of us at some point have felt this same way. The storm is raging and we see no way of escape. If we think about it, God had a captive audience in the hearts of these men. They had rowed to the middle of the Sea of Galilee. When they had departed earlier in the day, the weather was fine, but later it changed. It became violent, so much so that they feared for their lives. Jesus did not come to them until the fourth watch of the night. This means daybreak was not too far away. God waited to send His deliverance for a reason. As long as these men could row or manipulate their way across the water, they did not think they needed God. Even when the rain started, they probably felt as though they could handle the situation. But when the waves grew and began to billow into their boat and the wind howled and blew hard against their sails for a long period of time, they began to cry out. Still, Jesus waited to come to them until He was sure His coming would impact their lives. And it did!

"In the fourth watch of the night He came to them, walking on the sea. When the disciples saw Him walking on the sea, they were terrified, and said, 'It is a ghost!' And they cried out in fear. But immediately Jesus spoke to them saying, 'Take courage, it is I; do not be afraid'" (Matt. 14:22–27 NASB). You may feel you have entered the "fourth watch" of your night, and you wonder how and from where help will come. The prophet Isaiah has the answer. He wrote:

> Lift up your eyes on high and see who has created these stars, the One who leads forth their host by number, He calls them all by name; because of the greatness of His might and the strength of His power, not one of them is missing.
>
> Why do you say . . . "My way is hidden from the Lord, and

the justice due me escapes the notice of my God"? Do you not know? Have you not heard? The Everlasting God, the LORD, the Creator of the ends of the earth does not become weary or tired. His understanding is inscrutable. He gives strength to the weary, and to him who lacks might He increases power. (40:26–29 NASB)

You may be in a situation where you cannot walk away even for a few moments. You are tired and want to give up, but if you will trust Him in this travail, He will:

- give you His strength so you can continue.
- bring a sense of peace and quietness to your heart and mind.
- teach you how to trust Him in greater ways than you thought imaginable.
- show you how to anticipate the coming of His blessing and goodness.

God limits our suffering. He knows how much we can take and how much those we love can bear.

Wait, believing God's promises are true. There will be times when God requires you to do something that you really do not want to do. When your son or daughter is hurting, the last thing you want to hear is "let's wait a little longer." But often this is what we must do. God's timing is not our own, and we must realize that He has a reason for asking us to wait. It could be to strengthen our faith in Him, reveal an area of weakness that needs His attention, or simply to give us a season of rest before His answer comes. Regardless, the one thing we need to remember is waiting does not include passively sitting by and doing nothing. I have heard people say, "I can't just sit here and wait!" And I always say, "Yes, you can, because if you are waiting on God, you won't be just sitting around."

In times of waiting, God will motivate us to read and study His Word. Prayer also is essential every day; however, it is especially sweet and loving during times of waiting. This is when we need to hear God's voice of encouragement spoken to our hearts through His Word and the Holy Spirit. If the Lord wants you to wait for His best timing before you move ahead, then you must realize that He has something wonderful in store for you and those who are going through this long night with you. Waiting can result in a stronger relationship—with one another and more so with God. Be willing to wait for His timing and you will receive His very best.

Wait with expectation. Far too many people sense God leading them to wait for His open door and immediately assume the worst. This is very common when there is a loved one who is hurting and the doctor tells us we need to wait and see what happens next. Our thoughts can turn dark as we ask ourselves fear questions that God does not want us to consider: *What if it is too late? What if they do not know what they are doing? Are we wasting time? Are they telling me the whole story?*

One young father looked across the room at me and said, "I live with a constant knot in the pit of my stomach. I can't relax because I know that at any moment, the next shoe will drop and everything will be over." If we consider Christ's conversation with the disciples, we quickly understand that He never answered a single "What if" question. He wasn't waiting for the other shoe to drop because He was God and He knew exactly what was going to happen next and throughout eternity. After His resurrection, He asked them, "Why are you troubled, and why do doubts arise in your hearts?" (Luke 24:38 NASB). The very thing God promised would happen, did. Jesus rose from the grave. Is there ever a reason to doubt His ability and faithfulness? Another young father answered this question with great frustration over the loss of his son: "Jesus was God. My son was just that—my boy. How can I ever look at a sunrise again and have joy in my heart?" I told him that in time he would be able to through God's help and comfort.

We can get up each morning and go on because we know that no matter how great the pain seems within our hearts, He has a greater plan in mind for our sorrow. Our lives are slates waiting to be inscribed with words describing our faithfulness to God. Terminal illness, alcoholism, drugs, and physical abuse make no sense from our viewpoint. And yet, when our lives are turned toward Him, He promises to bring good out of even the worst circumstance. Therefore, we can get up every morning and continue. At first, it may be very painful, and we may feel a sense of guilt over going on with life. But this is exactly what brings glory to God— our desire to continue on and allow Him to heal the deep scars of sorrow, disappointment, and death that have been left behind.

Wait with a sense of knowing that God has a plan for the trial you are facing. The months and years David spent hiding out in caves and other places where Saul could not find him were times when he learned some of life's greatest lessons of faith. The same will be true for you as you trust God. As a young man, David wrote, "Even though I walk through the valley of the shadow of death, I fear no evil, for You are with me" (Ps. 23:4 NASB). He was not worried because he understood the God of the universe loved him and was the One who was watching over him. The same is true for you. Therefore, do not give up your hope. In Mark 9, a young boy was brought to Jesus for healing:

> The spirit threw him into a convulsion, and falling to the ground, he began rolling around and foaming at the mouth. And He asked the father, "How long has this been happening to him?" And he said, "From childhood. . . . But if You can do anything, take pity on us and help us!"
>
> And Jesus said to him, "'If You can? All things are possible to him who believes.' Immediately the boy's father cried out and said, "I do believe; help my unbelief." (vv. 20–24 NASB)

The Lord rebuked the evil spirit and then lifted the boy up. The first requirement for answered prayer is always belief. The second step involves acceptance. You must be willing to accept not only God's healing and restoration but also His sovereignty, because many times, healing may not take place on a physical level. It may happen on a much greater scale and be a testimony and witness to all who know you.

CHAPTER 5

Handling Your Fears

The man received a telephone call late in the afternoon telling him that his son had been in a horrible accident. "This is exactly what I had feared would happen." His face was white with panic as I entered the hospital waiting room to be with the family members. From his perspective, his worst fear had become a reality. He later admitted that he had spent years rehearsing that one moment. Secretly, he had carried this fear with him—a fear that was titled "What if my son has a horrible accident? What will I do?" At first, there was little I could say to help him because fear had such a stronghold on his emotions. Later, however, we talked about the incident and how his son had fully recovered.

"Ever since my son was young, I had a fear that one day something horrible would happen to him. I can remember the moment this thought came to mind. He was young and playing in the backyard. Suddenly, I remember thinking, *What would I do if he ever got hurt?* I also remember the feeling that gripped my heart. I tried to fight it off, but I couldn't because I was so afraid."

What is the one thing you fear the most? Could it be one of the five basic fears that at some point have plagued all of us: poverty, death, health problems, loss of a loved one, or failure? We probably could add at least two more to this list—loss of employment and fear of the future. All of us have little fears that we have to work through. However, every once in a while I run into a person who tells me, "I really do not have any fears." I never believe it. I'm not saying we should be fearful or that we should spend our lives in fear of what will happen in the future, but I do know that we live in a fallen world, and fear is one of the consequences. However, it did not exist until after Adam and Eve disobeyed God. This is where fear was born, and where mankind began to hide from God. Up to this point, Adam and Eve had enjoyed unbroken fellowship with the Lord. They had trusted God. He had provided for every need they had, and when He called to them, they had responded by rushing out to meet Him. Yet sin and fear changed this. "The LORD God called to the man, and said to him, 'Where are you?' [Adam] said, 'I heard the sound of You in the garden, and I was afraid" (Gen. 3:9, 10 NASB). Satan stood by enjoying the moment. He knew what he had accomplished through wickedness and sin.

A FEARFUL WORLD

We live in a society that is overrun with fear. And the news media fuels this blaze with one sinister report after another. Recently, I told the congregation at First Baptist Atlanta that I find it very difficult to watch or listen to the news. For one thing, you cannot believe what the media is reporting to you, and second, most of what is being said is being reported with another agenda in mind: to create fear within the hearts of those who are listening or watching. I have had people ask me, "Don't you want to know what is going on in the world?" And the answer is, of course I do. I want to keep up with world events. But since I have limited the amount of television I watch, I have not missed one single major news event. How could I? The reports are broadcast everywhere and often. You do not have to go far to find discouragement or despair because in many cases, it is a remote control click away.

We have chosen to fear the things of this world and not God. We are afraid to walk down a street at night in our own neighborhoods. We have alarm systems, security systems, and security guards. I remember a time when no one locked doors or windows. In fact, people would sleep with their windows open. Today, we are living in a society dominated by one question: "What if?" We fear for our safety; we're afraid of catching some dreadful disease, of financial loss, and of death. Fear can become so ingrained in people's lives that they cannot identify the source nor do they truly want to uncover the problem. They have talked themselves into believing that this is the way everyone lives. They are just a part of the pack. There is nothing wrong with being cautious. There is nothing wrong with making right choices and acting wisely, but there is a fine line between wisdom and fear. Many times the later masquerades itself as true concern, when in reality it is working diligently to prevent us from becoming the people God wants us to be.

As I stood in the hospital waiting room, I scanned the faces of those who had gathered to be with him. Most were etched with shock, worry, and fear. Only one face contained a look of deep concern but an even greater look of trust and peace. It was the boy's mother's face. *Was she in shock?* I wondered. *Does she really love him?* Everyone else was one step away from sheer panic, but this dear lady had requested that we join hands and pray. "No one can help my son but the Lord," she said softly. Suddenly, I recalled John's words: "There is no fear in love; but perfect love casts out fear" (1 John 4:18 NASB). Could the others in the room experience this same sense of peace and calm? Yes, but it was a choice they needed to make.

Some accidents happen so suddenly that we cannot help but feel fearful. Our pulse rate increases along with our breathing, and we suddenly wonder why our legs will not hold us up any longer. All of this is an expected response to sudden bad news. The problem comes if days later we cannot shake the gripping sense of fear that has settled over our lives. A growing number of families are dealing with situations that involve Post

Traumatic Stress syndrome as a result of the war in the Middle East. Like those who went through the tragedy of September 11, recovery can take a long time. Sons and daughters are returning home from the battlefield and, in many cases, continue to fight horrendous emotional battles. While this has been true of every war we have fought, knowing that does not relieve the anxiety, fear, or pressure our soldiers feel. I found one private's confession very interesting. "I want to go back," he said. "I've signed up for another tour because the only people who understand how I feel are over there." How many of us have been in a spiritual battle and felt this same way? We look for someone who can identify with our plight, but the one thing we don't want to do is to look for a person who will fan the flames of fear in our life. Many things can be devastating to the Christian life, but few are as deadly as fear. This is because few things have the ability to make us as vulnerable as fear does.

"The first time my son had a seizure, I didn't know what to do." The mother said. "We wanted to deny them, but deep inside we knew they were here to stay for a while and we were afraid. I think some of my running and overcompensation was an effort to curb the fear I was feeling. If I stopped, I would have to accept the truth, and I was not ready to do that. I wanted God to kill the giant with one stone. I believed that eventually He would do that, but in the meantime, I loaded up my emotional basket with as many stones as I could gather. I was determined to take that giant out, if I could, on my own!"

At a critical time in Israel's history, God spoke the following words to a nation that was under the siege of fear. I believe these are just as applicable today, especially when dealing with fear, doubt, and anxiety: "Do not fear, for I am with you; do not anxiously look about you, for I am your God. I will strengthen you, surely I will help you, surely I will uphold you with My righteous right hand" (Isa. 41:10 NASB).

I have listed several dates beside this verse in my Bible. I cannot remember what many of these represent, but they probably mark times when I felt fearful and alone. God in His loving mercy understood my weakness and led me to read this passage. It was His personal word of hope to me in a particularly difficult situation. If we are going to deal with fear, we must be willing to ask ourselves some pretty tough questions. For one, we need to uncover the source of our fear. What happened to create such a deadly sense of fear within our hearts? Was it news like the woman received whose son suddenly started having seizures? Or is it a vague sense of fear like the man at the beginning of this chapter experienced for a long time? Fear can wear a person down—physically, emotionally, and spiritually.

You may think, *My son or daughter is hurting and I don't know what will happen next. We have received reports, but no one knows the outcome. I have a right to be fearful. After all, I have prayed and prayed, but it seems that God is silent—still—and not talking. I'm scared. Even though I know it is wrong to feel this way, I do. I'm a Christian and should know better.* Before you can deal with fear, you must uncover the source and at the same time realize that God loves you right where you are. He is not looking for you to perform a certain way. But He doesn't want you to be entrapped by fear because He knows it is debilitating and will prevent you from seeing clearly the road He has for you to travel. It may be a rough and narrow path. However, when your thoughts turn fearful, you cannot focus on anything but the trial and tragedy. The one thing your child needs in times of crisis is the truth of God. The situation may be very severe, but there is always hope through Jesus Christ, if not for this lifetime, then for the one that we will live with Him forever.

GOD'S OFFER TO US

God has a challenge He wants to extend to us, one of trust where we commit ourselves to abiding in His care regardless of our circumstances or the outcome of our situation. "I can't let go," one mother said with tears. "I know I should be able to trust Jesus, but my baby is hurting and I just can't let go." As hard and as difficult as this may seem, we must come to a point where we let God be God in the lives of our children. Fear, which is the polar opposite of faith, shouts for us to cling to them even tighter. But God calls us to open up our hands and allow Him to work in our lives and the lives of those we love. He uses pain and sorrow to do a great work of love. We must be willing for Him to go to work. Is it better for us never to experience trial or heartache than have the extreme privilege of watching Him work miraculously on our behalf? I certainly do not believe this for my own life. The times that I have grown the most have also been the most painful and trying.

By the time Paul wrote First Timothy, it was obvious to him that his young protégé was struggling. The ministry was difficult in Ephesus, which was known for its widely practiced paganism and immorality. Sin-rich environments such as this one could wear a pastor down and leave him longing to step away from the ministry. Paul knew he had to act quickly or Timothy could become extremely discouraged. He wrote a letter that not only turned out to be an encouragement for Timothy but for us as well. "For I am mindful of the sincere faith within you, which first dwelt in your grandmother Lois and your mother Eunice, and I am sure that it is in you as well. For this reason I remind you to kindle afresh the gift of God which is in you through the laying on of my hands. For God has not given us a spirit of timidity, but of power and love and discipline" (2 Tim. 1:5–7 NASB). God understands our suffering, but He still offers us an opportunity to learn more about Him and to experience His love in a greater way than we could if we were living without difficulty and trial. We get to live out our faith. It becomes real rather than something that we talk about hypothetically.

Timothy had an opportunity like this. His assignment was tough. So tough, in fact, it appeared he was about to give up. He was losing his confidence, and Paul wrote admonishing him to stay the course by rekindling the faith in God that he learned as a child. Faith is essential to overcoming fear. You may have received very bad news and the shock has left you feeling so fearful that you cannot relax. Your children need you, but you are stuck in a cycle of fear as you wonder what could be next on the horizon. Maintaining a fixed focus on Jesus Christ will change this quickly. You may still feel sorrowful, but when you have the right focus, you will also have hope for the future. The enemy wants you to believe it is all over. But his dead end is actually God's new beginning.

There will be times when you must make a choice as to how you will live: fearful, cowering, and wondering what bad thing will happen next, or victorious because you serve a risen Savior who loves you with an everlasting love and who has promised to never leave or abandon you (Deut. 31:6, 8). Perhaps the circumstances of life have narrowed your focus. Disappointment has robbed you of joy. Dread and uncertainty have refueled your growing fears, and you now wonder why life has turned out so differently than what you planned. While there is no way to avoid fear completely, you can learn how to handle it correctly. You must understand the difference between godly fear and a protective fear.

Godly fear is a way to reverence the Lord. God instructs us to worship Him, but unless we understand something about His awesome nature, we will not know how to do this. We will view Him as being an object of fear rather than being the basis for our worship and love. There is nothing within Him that should cause fear and dread in our lives. Even when a child we love is sick or threatened by a deadly disease, we should be able to say with Job, "As for me, I know that my Redeemer lives" (19:25 NASB). If our hearts are filled with fear, we may know the words, but we don't see Him as our Redeemer and Lord, the one Person who loves us and wants to comfort our deepest hurts. We fear Him, but we don't reverence Him. We dread His coming the way Adam and Eve did, and we want to run away from Him. This is exactly what Satan wants us to do because he knows that on our own, we will only experience greater heartache and sorrow.

A reverent fear motivates us to acknowledge God's holiness and honor His ways. Moses wrote, "Now, Israel, what does the LORD your God require from you, but to fear the LORD your God, to walk in all His ways and love Him, and to serve the LORD your God with all your heart and with all your soul" (Deut. 10:12 NASB). We should not be afraid of God in the same way that we fear evil. He is a God of righteousness, holiness, and justice. He also is a God of love, mercy, and grace, who has chosen to save us from an eternal death by sending His Son to die on the cross for our sins. There is no greater love than the love God has for us. And these are the very reasons we bow our heads in prayer and worship to Him. He is to be honored because He is the God of the universe. No one is over Him. But He never intends for us to be afraid of Him and this is exactly what fear persuaded Adam and Eve to do. At the sound of His voice, they hid in fear of what He would do because they had sinned. Even before sin had left its mark on their lives, the Lord knew they would yield to temptation. It was His love for His creation that motivated Him to establish a plan for mankind's restoration.

God gives us a protective sense of fear. This is the type of fear that warns us when we are about to do something that is wrong and deadly. We have a sense of protective fear when it comes to our children. This is why we hold their hands, walk closely beside them, and talk to them about life's trials. It is a legitimate fear that helps us establish healthy boundaries. God has a protective fear for each one of us. This is why He has given us certain commandments and principles to live by. For example, if we find ourselves in a situation that compromises our safety or who we are as a believer, an alarm should go off inside. When it comes to our children, we tell them not to touch a hot stove because they will get burned. Experience has taught us that this is true. Protective fear shouts a valid warning. However, many times a parent will end up teaching his child to be "fearful" instead of just careful. Over time, the fear can turn into a phobia—something that Satan can use to prevent us from experiencing life to the fullest.

Before you say no to the opportunities and events God brings your way beyond your normal routine, stop and ask if the fear you are feeling is legitimate or illegitimate. When we are fearful, we can list a bounty of reasons why we should not step out on faith and trust God. Most of the time, we can come up with a reason why our fear appears quite biblical in nature. The truth is, God does not want us to become afraid and cower away from those we love, and most of all, away from Him. He "has not given us a spirit of fear, but . . . of love and of a sound mind" (2 Tim. 1:7 NKJV).

THE REASONS WE BECOME FEARFUL

Years ago I ran into an old friend I had not seen in a long time. We sat down to talk in an area that contained a balcony. After a while, I decided to stand up and walk over to the railing and look down. We were up about twenty floors. My friend immediately jumped up and said, "Don't get too close." I asked, "Why not?" And he replied, "I'm afraid of high places!" He later confessed that he had been afraid of heights since he was young. His mother would always caution him not to get too close to the edge of anything that was high. "You might fall over the side and die," she would tell him. As a result of her words, he grew up believing that being too close to the edge of anything was dangerous. Over the years, his fear expanded. He hated to fly, couldn't tolerate the thought of hiking in the mountains, and loathed balconies at hotels. Feeling fearful for the wrong reasons can play into the enemy's hand and leave us wondering why others are enjoying life to such a great degree.

Not all fear is real. In fact, more than half of the things we fear will never come true. There are times when we become fearful over situations that just do not exist and never will. Most of the fears we feel are not real—they are imagined or incorrectly perceived. What are the causes of fear?

We are taught to be fearful when we are young. Our parents can actually instill fear into our lives. One father told his daughter that she did not have to go to college. He had tried it and came home after several semesters telling friends and relatives that he was just not college material. Before her death, his mother had told him to be careful, not to take too many risks, and just play it safe or something unthinkable could happen. When she died, the "unthinkable" did happen and he could not recover. The young man grew up with a sense of fear and dread. His entire life was spent dodging opportunities that he felt could bring pain or displeasure.

You do not have to settle for a life lived in fear. You can break free of its grasp, but you must decide to take the first step of faith. And the truth is this: Those who are hurting need to know that there is hope beyond all of the clutter and brokenness this world offers. This is why the apostle Paul wrote, "I can do all things through Him who strengthens me" (Phil. 4:13 NASB). He was not afraid, and yet he lived every day with the threat of death. Lay aside your deepest fears and ask God to live His life through you so you can be a minister of hope to those who are in hopeless situations.

We are ignorant about our circumstances. For years, I have heard people say that information is powerful. I certainly believe this, especially when it comes to exposing fear. The very fact that God has given us a spirit of love and power says that we have the ability to move past fear and any depression that comes with it. As a believer you can ask Him to give you the ability to discern the truth about the situation that you are facing, whether it involves your children or yourself.

In writing this book, my first thought was to discuss situations where children are hurting due to disease, but there are so many other ways for hurt to come into our lives. Drugs, alcoholism, and sexual abuse are just three more ways the lives of our children can be torn apart. When this happens, parents often wonder where they went wrong and if they could have done something to prevent this from happening. This is not always true. Many times, Satan will tempt us to feel guilty or shameful over things that we cannot control. Therefore, the best thing to do whenever we sense the enemy tempting to make us feel guilty is to ask God to give us His perspective of our circumstances.

We have a fearful imagination. Once again, the world and its media have tried to program us into believing the worst will happen. Bad things do come our way. Children become sick. We struggle to be in control of our emotions and circumstances, but the majority of what we feel is just not true and it never will come true. One young woman in her early twenties told me how she was afraid that something bad would happen to her husband and son. She was not living life because every day was a countdown to the end. This is a terrible way to waste the life God has given us.

We doubt the unchanging promises of God. When we take God out of the equation, we set ourselves up for failure. The psalmist wrote: "Trust in the LORD and do good; dwell in the land and cultivate faithfulness. Delight yourself in the LORD; and He will give you the desires of your heart. Commit your way to the LORD, trust also in Him, and He will do it. He will bring forth your righteousness as the light" (37:3–6 NASB). The author of Proverbs reminds us to "trust in the LORD with all your heart and do not lean on your own understanding. In all your ways acknowledge Him, and He will make your paths straight" (3:5, 6).

God has promised to lead and guide us. But we must be still enough to hear His voice. This means focusing on God and not the fears that we feel. He has promised He will always be with us. Therefore, we do not need to be anxious about anything (Isa. 41:10). He reminds us that He is our refuge and strength (Ps. 18). Feelings are just that, feelings that may or may not be true. However, if we set the focus of our hearts on the unchanging truth of God's Word and His faithfulness, our fearful perspective will change. Peter did great walking on the water to Jesus. He would have made it to the Savior if he had not become fearful.

When he first got out of the boat, his gaze was set on one thing: Jesus. Halfway there, he noticed the waves crashing around him and suddenly he realized what he was doing and began to sink. "Seeing the wind, he became frightened, and beginning to sink, he cried out, 'LORD, save me!' Immediately Jesus stretched out His hand and took hold of him, and said to him, 'You of little faith, why did you doubt?' When they got into the boat, the wind stopped" (Matt. 14:30–32 NASB). But you do not have to succumb to fear. In fact, after the resurrection, he no longer walked through life fearing tomorrow. He had the hope of the living God within Him, and you can have the same thing. No matter what your circumstances may be, you can roll your burden onto Jesus, and He will give you comfort and rest (Matt. 11:28).

THE CONSEQUENCES OF LIVING WITH FEAR

Fear has many consequences, but the one that stands out the most is how it prevents us from being all that we need to be to those who are hurting. As painful as it may seem, in the process of living with hurt and discovering the goodness of God, we must move beyond fear to faith or we will sink into depression. The greater risk is that we could easily take others down with us. This is why it is crucial to read a passage of Scripture from God's Word each day. In my own life, I have often found courage to continue through reading the Psalms. There have been times when I did feel lonely, fearful, and not sure about the future, but then I would read something that David had written and I would suddenly sense the hope of God welling up deep within me:

> The LORD is my light and my salvation; whom shall I fear? The LORD is the defense of my life; whom shall I dread? . . . Though a host encamp against me, my heart will not fear; though war arise against me, in spite of this I shall be confident. One thing I have asked from the LORD . . . that I may dwell in the house of the LORD all the days of my life, to behold the beauty of the LORD and to meditate in His temple. For in the day of trouble He will conceal me in His tabernacle; in the secret place of His tent He will hide me. (27:1, 3–5 NASB)

David was in the throes of death. His life was in jeopardy, but his heart was set on God. He was fearless in his faith.

Fear can stifle our capacity to think and act properly. When we are only focused on what we think can go wrong, it usually does. When our minds are set like flints on listening to God, laying everything out before Him in prayer and trusting Him for a solution, doors open that we thought would be closed. Loved ones receive treatment and care that we never believed would come, and beyond all of this, we have a hope growing inside of us that is the result of God's intimate love. We actually can sense His nearness because our hearts are locked up with Him and not lost in our fears.

Fear can result in indecision. When a person's mind is overcome by fearful words and thoughts, he cannot make a wise decision. Each one of us can feel panic rising and wonder what we should do. When this happens, we need to step back from our circumstance, even if it is only for a few minutes, and ask God to give us clarity and wisdom. Instead of rushing one way in our thinking and then jumping off to follow another mental trail of fear, we should sit down with God and an open Bible and pray, "Lord, show me Your truth. Give me Your courage and understanding. I feel alone in all of this, but You are with me."

Fear diminishes our ability to achieve. Just like the man who came home from college because he was afraid he would fail all of his classes, fear derails our hope and interest for others. We cannot be ministers of His truth if we doubt His goodness. If we cave into fear, we miss the blessing He has for us even in painful times. Old saints of God would talk about "rolling the trouble of the hearts over on to God." The chorus of the hymn "At the Cross" helps us understand this concept: "At the cross, at the cross where I first saw the light, and the burden of my heart rolled away, it was there by faith I received my sight, and now I am happy all the day!" There is a way to experience a deep sense of joy and contentment even in times of horrendous adversity, but it is only through the loving care of the Savior that we can do this. Never feel guilty for sensing His extreme love for you. It is given to strengthen you along your way through the valley.

Fear causes panic. God tells us to be still and know that He is God. He is over all things. He is omniscient (all-knowing), omnipotent (all-powerful), and omnipresent (always with us). There is never a moment that we are outside His eternal care. Fear, however, tempts us into thinking that God is not aware of our condition or that He does not care. The truth is, He cares very much and He has a plan that He is going to put into operation. Panic, however, can motivate us to launch out on our own without God's guidance. We can become so fearful that we think we must do something or nothing will be done.

Timing is extremely important to God. He waited to come to the disciples who were caught in a horrendous storm on the Sea of Galilee until the fourth watch of the night. He knew exactly what He was doing. He also waited to go to Bethany until after Lazarus died. What sense did that make? It made no sense from a human standpoint, but from God's perspective, it made perfect sense. He knows exactly what He is doing and we can trust Him wherever He leads us, even when the way before us appears dark and foreboding. It never really is because Jesus is always in the boat with us. We do not have to panic because God has promised to calm the storm that rages against us.

Fear damages our relationship with others. Panic usually includes such a rush of emotion that we do not have the ability to think clearly about how our frantic words and actions affect others. We are so focused on our need, our problem, our hurt, and our pain that we have trouble hearing God's words of reassurance. I have actually heard people talk about searching through the Bible looking for some word of hope. Their pace is so accelerated that there is no way for them to exercise any faith. In fact, faith is not their principle concern. They simply want an answer and they want it now.

The woman whose son suddenly began having seizures finally understood that her search would not take her any further than God wanted her to go. In other words, she could call every doctor in the book, but she would not land on the right one until He was ready for the answer to be found. This is why it is so important to learn how to rest in the Lord and trust Him in times of difficulty. He sees everything. He knows the pain your child is experiencing and He has an answer, but you must be still enough to hear it. "I'm convinced that I missed God's best for us at the time," the woman continued. "I learned a great deal, but if I had to do it all over again, my prayer would be to pray and then to wait for God to open the door. However, even in our bumbling attempt to gain an answer to our son's problem, He was still at work."

Fear steals our peace, joy, and contentment. None of these can coexist with fear. If we do not get hold of our emotions by allowing God to take control of the situation, we could run the risk of losing our witness and testimony. One young woman, who spent six years battling cancer, told her mom that the only thing that really mattered was her witness for Jesus Christ. Sometimes children have much more insight into the ways of God than adults do. This was the case in this young girl's life. Her parents were so devastated by the entire process of dealing with cancer that they did not even want to talk about her treatment. Cancer had the opposite effect on their daughter. Her only concern was what she could do to encourage those around her to trust the Savior. Her love for God was so great and evident that nurses and doctors were moved with emotion by her faith. No one felt sorry for her, but everyone she met wanted to know how she could be so happy. She never hesitated to say it was because of the love she felt from Jesus.

When you trust God with your life and the lives of those you love, you will be able to rest in His omnipotent care. It is in these abiding times that you also learn about His ways, including the depth of love He has for you. There is no way to do this when you are running around frantic and worried about what may or may not happen tomorrow. He commands us to "Be still, and know" that He is God (Ps. 46:10 NIV). He also says, "In quietness and trust is your strength" (Isa. 30:15 NIV).

PUTTING ASIDE FEAR

If this is true, then how do we overcome fear? Is there a formula that we can apply to our lives that will bring hope and a sense of direction, especially when the storms of life strike suddenly and without warning?

First, you need to acknowledge that you are afraid. There is nothing wrong with telling God that you are frightened. He already knows the truth. He understands the impact that a hurting child can have on your life. It does not matter if your son or daughter is three months or thirty-three years old. They belong to us, and whenever they struggle we hurt for them. One woman came up to me at the end of a church service and requested prayer for her older son, who was addicted to drugs. She kept saying, "I am so afraid that something really bad is going to happen." She could not get past her fear or the panic she felt. Consequently, she was tired and could not really pray for her son the way she would like to pray. I told her that God loved her son even more than she did. To see her son free of this addiction, she would have to let go of him. Many times we cling to the very thing that we are afraid of losing. Allowing God to bear our burdens requires a tremendous step of faith, but there is no other way to live this life other than by faith.

The second thing you want to do is ask God to help you identify the source of your fear. Do you have a problem letting go because you are afraid that you will no longer be in control of your circumstances? Many people cling to their problems as if they had the power to change them and they don't—at least not on their own. Successful change always requires acceptance. We must be willing to let God show us where we have failed. "If I let go, something bad may happen," one man told me. I considered his remarks carefully since I knew that his marriage was falling apart as a result of his daughter's death. "I can't give God that much control. Not now, maybe not ever." I understood that he had been through serious trauma and the last thing he needed was someone telling him the consequences of his need for control. Instead, I reminded him of God's unconditional love and the fact that while we cannot understand all of life's sorrows, we can trust God to show us exactly how to live each day. This is a promise that I believe is true regardless of the level of our faith. Remember, He is always faithful, even when we are faithless.

The third thing you need to do is acknowledge you need God's help. You may not have the emotional strength to believe that He will work fully on your behalf. However, if you will take even a small step of faith, you will find that He is ever faithful. The psalmist wrote, "To the faithful you show yourself faithful" (Ps. 18:25 NIV). In Psalm 40, he wrote, "I waited patiently for the LORD; he turned to me and heard my cry. He lifted me out of the slimy pit, out of the mud and mire; he set my feet on a rock and gave me a firm place to stand. He put a new song in my mouth, a hymn of praise to our God" (vv. 1–3 NIV).

The fourth thing you need to do is change your focus from one of fear and worry to one of faith and praise. God tells us to "cease striving and know that I am God" (Ps. 46:10 NASB). All of our rushing around will never solve a single problem that could not be solved much easier, and many times quicker, than through prayer. If our focus is set solely on what we can do in our own strength or what others can do for us, then we will face disappointment. There may be some things that work out along the way, but the stress level will be much higher than if we set the focus of our hearts on the Lord and His ability. This does not mean that we are to abandon the advice of professionals He brings into our lives. It does mean that until we place God in the right position, which is the center of our lives, we will become frustrated and weary. On an even greater personal level, you will miss the blessing of developing a close, personal relationship with Jesus Christ. You can know Him as your Savior, but do you know Him as Lord?

You may ask, "What if He tells me no?" Or, "What would I do if something bad happens?" Let me ask you this: how can you prevent the God of this universe from doing exactly what He wants to do? You can't. But the one thing you can do is open yourself up to His unconditional love and allow Him to pour out His understanding in your life so that you will have all the knowledge you need to go forward. One of the best things that comes from knowing God is this: You no longer have to live in fear. When holy, righteous God is fighting for you, you will have the very best you could ever hope to have. Fear fades when exposed to the light of God's truth and goodness.

CHAPTER 6

Help for the Hurting

All of us must handle hurt at different stages in life for different reasons. One of the deepest hurts we experience is the emotional pain that comes from watching our children hurt. I believe the author of Hebrews gives us a very encouraging message— one the Lord has used in my own life to bring comfort and hope during times of severe trial and heartache. He writes:

Nothing in all creation is hidden from God's sight. Everything is uncovered and laid bare before the eyes of him to whom we must give account. Therefore, since we have a great high priest who has gone through the heavens, Jesus the Son of God, let us hold firmly to the faith we profess. For we do not have a high priest who is unable to sympathize with our weaknesses, but we have one who has been tempted [tested and tried] in every way, just as we are—yet was without sin. Let us then approach the throne of grace with confidence, so that we may receive mercy and find grace to help us in our time of need. (4:13–16 NIV)

Feelings of intense hurt can come as the result of physical trauma, emotional or mental stress, and spiritual anguish. The emotional darkness that comes from suffering can become so foreboding that we may wonder if we will ever see a hopeful light again. The answer is, "Yes, we will." When I have gone through a difficult season or watched others fight feelings of discouragement, I am constantly reminded of David's words in Psalm 23, "Even though I walk through the valley of the shadow of death, I fear no evil, for You are with me" (v. 4 NASB). The one thing that creates a sense of safety for us is the fact that we are not alone. God is walking with us. He abides with us, which means He stays with us through difficulty, trials, and confusion, as well as times filled with joy and fulfillment.

I realize there are people who "will" themselves into believing that they can make it through anything. But I can honestly say I would never want to work through a single trial without God. Walking through emotional darkness can be overwhelming when you feel alone and as if no one understands your circumstances. I know what it is like to be tempted to feel hopeless and frightened. No one is exempt from experiencing either one of these. However, there is always hope because God is with us. He offers a way through the darkness because He knows the best path for us to take. He is eternal and He is in control of all things. The lost man will experience a sense of true hopelessness because he does not have an anchor for his soul. He is drifting out on an open sea, vulnerable to storms and searing heat. The moment he realizes the nature of his condition and calls out to God, he is given the greatest source of help that he could ever hope to have. I do not know how people get through severe trials apart from the love and support of God.

FROM LITTLE FAITH TO GREAT FAITH

You may be a Christian and still you are battling thoughts of depression. You have stood at a distance and watched a group of doctors walk toward you. You can sense from the look on their faces that the news is not good. You feel as though your life is breaking apart and the cry of your heart is, "God, why? Is there a way for You to remove this painful situation?" There are times when we must go through a season of darkness—times spent in emotional and physical valleys—in order to enjoy the goodness of God's great love. This is not a simple or trite statement. During the process of working through our disappointment and anger over our circumstances, we should begin to realize that God plans to use us for a greater purpose.

He wants you to come to a point where you trust Him fully. In other words, you stop questioning His ability and walk through the valley leaning only on Him. The suffering we encounter can bring tremendous results, especially when our lives are surrendered to God. You may ask, "How can this be true? My daughter is battling alcoholism, and I don't see how God can use this sort of thing." He can and He does. He uses our trials to teach us how to trust Him to a greater degree. We need to remember three things in times of great stress: God loves us, God has a plan, and God will never abandon you (Ps. 94:14; 1 Sam. 12:22). He wants you to learn to step back and not be so intent on rushing forward. If there is a need to move quickly, He will make this clear. The way before you may seem difficult, but when God is involved, it will be one you can navigate easily. The very pain you experience is the same heartache that is being felt by others. The potential is very great for your life and situation to be used by God to encourage others who are struggling. When trouble first hits, this is usually the last thing on our minds. However, once we open our hearts to God's goodness, we find that we suddenly want to tell as many people as possible about the hope we have inside.

God knows we need His strength and help. There are so many people who do not have anyone to talk to about the emotional and mental pain they are experiencing as a result of watching their children battle sickness and disease. Hospitals and other organizations have set up Web sites and online discussions just to facilitate this need. While a Web site or an e-mail group may offer a certain degree of support, nothing can replace the caring look of a friend or an understanding hug that comes from someone who has stood in your shoes or a knowing look of a fellow sufferer. Even greater than these is the loving reassurance God offers us.

Some of the people who read this book may feel as though no one understands their loneliness. They long to express their feelings, hurt, and heartache without fear of being rejected, condemned, shut out, isolated, criticized, or judged. There is always a safe place with Jesus. He understands our feelings of rejection and the deep need we have at times to protect ourselves. While opinions have changed with time, many of the families whose children are dying with incurable diseases such as AIDS still feel as though they have no one they can turn to for help. They battle guilt and regret, along with deep sorrow—sorrow so deep it cannot be easily expressed. However, nothing is too difficult for God to understand. He knows everything, and He loves each person with an everlasting love. He also has sent His Holy Spirit to comfort and remind you of His personal promises. This is your greatest hope—the hope you have in Jesus Christ.

JESUS IDENTIFIES WITH OUR DEEPEST NEED

God understands the stress that comes from watching our children struggle. We may feel that we are given very little insight into His feelings as He watched His Son die on the cross. However, the torture Christ felt on the cross was greater than anything we have ever experienced. Nothing could come close to His pain, and nothing compares to the agony God felt over the death of His Son. There had to be redemptive value in the cross or Jesus' suffering would have been in vain. Jesus Christ perfectly understands our hurts. "We do not have a high priest who cannot sympathize with our weaknesses, but One who has been tempted in all things as we are, yet without sin" (Heb. 4:15 NASB). He understands what we are thinking because He wrapped Himself in human flesh and came into this world. He loved us so much that He wanted to identify with us. This is part of what the author of Hebrews is saying: God loves us and wants us to know that He understands how we feel. Therefore, He put aside His royal robe and took on the cloak of humanity. He was still God, but He also was human and that part of Him experienced a greater hurt than we will ever know. He can identify with our fears, frustrations, and anxieties, though He never gave into the temptation to doubt God's purpose and plan. We can draw near to Him because He knows our struggle.

I want to make something very clear: When you feel as though you are alone and no one cares, Jesus Christ does. It is impossible for a child of God to be alone. Yet over the years, I have received calls from believers who feel as though no one cares. Years ago when our children were young, my wife and I felt it was important to give them some added responsibility around the house. They already had certain chores that they were doing, but they were old enough to do a little more. One day I asked Andy to help me in the yard. He immediately became excited and couldn't wait for us to begin. We went outside, and I told him that I was going to teach him how to weed the flower beds. We got down on our hands and knees and began working down one side of the house. I remember that we talked about all kinds of things. He asked questions and wanted to know if he was doing his job right.

After a while, I got up and inspected what we had done and realized he had a handle on what we were doing. I told him, "You keep weeding until you get to the end of the house and I'm going to get the lawn mower and begin cutting the grass."

I walked to the backyard and was opening the shed to pull the mower out and get a couple of other things when I heard a noise behind me. I turned around only to find Andy standing behind me. "Did you finish weeding?" I asked.

He nodded yes and then asked, "What are you doing in here?"

I answered, "Getting the lawn mower ready." Then I said, "Let's take a look at what you have done." But he replied, "Can I help?"

It was then that I realized something I should have known all along: Andy wasn't excited about doing yard work; he was excited about being with me. Up to that point, the things we had given him to do were things he had to do alone. He didn't dislike pulling up weeds; he just did not want to be alone. We ended up spending a lot of time together that day. God wants you to desire His fellowship above all else. He wants to be with you, and He longs for you to want the same thing of Him. Really, there is nothing in life that we do alone. We may tell ourselves that we have no one beside us, but God is there and He is not walking away. He doesn't leave even for a few minutes. You will never have to search for Him or ask Him if you can help.

He has given you His Spirit—the Holy Spirit—as a comforter and guide.

A Shelter in the Storm

For years I have watched people fight with feelings of guilt. This feeling can surface after a loved one has been diagnosed with a serious illness. It can also come in the aftermath of a sudden injury. The person who is hurting needs support and reassurance, but those closest to him or her begin struggling with feelings of guilt and avoid going to see their son or daughter or other family member. All this does is deepen the hurt. It creates a wall between those who have a true need and those who should be able to be supportive.

Denial is another reason family members may find it hard to go to the hospital to be with those who are hurting. They may go only to find excuses for not returning or for not staying for a long period of time. They don't want to face the inevitable, which is the serious nature of the situation and the responsibility this may bring. I have received cards from church members simply saying, "Thank you for coming." My visit as a pastor registered that I cared.

We also need to realize that God may actually prevent some people from being a part of our lives, especially if He knows their reactions will not be honoring to Him. Some people are motivated by guilt. They really are not conscious of our needs and feel guilty for not supporting us better. But God may not prompt them to make the effort to visit or call. I'm convinced that those who are too busy to pray or get involved are often the ones who miss a great blessing. In times of stress and increased pressure, you only want what He wants for you and your family. In other words, keep a loving check on your heart. Allow Him to bring those across your path who will cheer you on and also pray for you. The woman who "could not face" her brother in the hospital was only thinking about herself and not about the blessing she could be if she surrendered her life for God to use.

Week after week, we sit next to people in church who are hurting, but we fail to engage them in any real conversation. Their lives are a mess and their children are on drugs or have left home. They don't know what to do, and they are afraid to tell anyone for fear that they will be scolded, shunned, or reprimanded. As a Christian community, we should be brokenhearted over the way we have treated others. In favor of our own desires, we have disregarded the needs of others and missed the opportunity to demonstrate God's love to someone who is hurting. If you are unsaved and you are living with feelings of despair and hopelessness, you may be tempted to give up. I want to encourage you to turn to Christ where you will find help and also someone who will love and accept you no matter what wrong turns you have taken in this life. God's answer is always yes:

- Yes, He will save you.
- Yes, there is hope—even when you feel hopeless.
- Yes, you can have a future, whether short or long, and you can impact this world for good and not evil.

- Yes, you can leave behind feelings of depression and learn how to live for today and encourage others who are fighting the same battle as you.

Jesus will never say, "Don't come to Me. I have heard all of this before." He is merciful, and He is with you for the long haul. That means if it takes a lifetime, He is willing to stay at your side. Now, there may be times that you choose to disobey Him or step away from His will. While His love for you continues, He also allows the consequence of sin to impact your life. He loves you, but He also will discipline you. He does this to draw you back to Himself. But even in times of discipline, God continues to proclaim His love for us: "The Lord disciplines those he loves, and he punishes everyone he accepts as a son [or daughter]" (Heb. 12:6 NIV). His discipline is not like the world's punishment. His goal is not to harm or shame you. It is to guide and prevent you from straying off the path He has chosen for you to take. There will be times when we feel shame over our actions, especially if they involve sin. However, God restores us and forgives us when we confess that what we have done is wrong and make a decision to turn away from our sinful behavior. Anyone, who is living in a sinful situation, should take these measures:

Confess your sin to God. You may have to suffer the consequences of your actions, but He has promised to forgive you and restore your fellowship with Him (1 John 1:9).

Separate yourself from sin. If this means moving out, then pack up and go. I'm not talking about those who are already married. I'm strictly addressing those who are single and living in immorality. You cannot live in sin and enjoy God's goodness at the same time. One young man told me that he did not believe this. He was so sure of himself. Several months later, he returned with a totally different story. He felt as though God had left him, and he did not know how to return to the Lord because of the shame he felt.

Receive God's forgiveness. Many of the people I have talked with over the years have a hard time forgiving themselves even though they may know God loves them.

Make a commitment to live for Him. When we decide that we are going to live for the Lord regardless of our circumstances, something within us changes. Suddenly, we gain a sense of peace and stability. In times of great trial, it is especially important to draw even nearer to the Lord. When we are weary, tired from trying, and overwhelmed by life's struggles, we are the most vulnerable to Satan's assault. In good times, when we falsely believe the enemy can't harm us, we may drop our guard and end up yielding to sin. This can happen to a greater degree to those who have been fighting the fight of faith for a long time.

Years ago I watched a young family come apart at the seams after their daughter was involved in a terrible automobile crash. At first, the husband and wife clung to one another and to God. However, after it became evident their daughter would not recover, they began shutting off from one another. They had other children to consider, but this did not seem to matter. All they could think about was how this had affected their lives. They had dealt with other tragedies, and I felt as though they were spiritually exhausted. When I pointed this out, they rebuked me, saying that they were fine. A month later they had isolated themselves away from family and friends. They also had done the same thing to one another. This is when they began blaming one another for their daughter's accident. Everyone in this family was hurting. I wish I could write that their marriage survived, but it didn't. Not because God wanted it to fail, but because in their personal anger and grief, they made a conscious decision to turn away from Him and from one another.

Life is a series of choices. God has mapped out a route for us to travel through the storms of life. However, at any time, we can refuse to take the road He has opened before us. We may not like it. It may appear rocky and even foreboding, but we will not walk alone. The moment we begin to sink into selfish thoughts is the moment we have taken the first step toward failure. Especially in times of great trial, it is crucial for us to focus only on Christ. Whatever it takes to accomplish this, we need to do it. Dropping our guard and thinking about how difficult our circumstances are lead to one place—spiritual failure and emotional unrest. The psalmist wrote:

God is our refuge and strength, a very present help in trouble. Therefore we will not fear, though the earth should change and though the mountains slip into the heart of the sea; though its waters roar and foam, though the mountains quake at its swelling pride. Selah. There is a river whose streams make glad the city of God, the holy dwelling places of the Most High. God is in the midst of her, she will not be moved; God will help her when morning dawns. (46:1–5 NASB)

The woman with the sick son paused in telling her story long enough to reflect on her feelings during that very stressful time. "It was sometime during the first couple of years that we were searching for an answer to the reason my son was having seizures that I realized what I needed to do. It took a long time for me to do it, but I finally decided it was the only way to survive the storm that had broken over my family. I needed to bind myself to God. There was no other way, even though I looked for one. All the roads I took looking for the right answer led me back to God. The bigger questions became 'Could I trust Him?' and 'Was He really on my side?'" At some point, each one of us has asked these or similar questions. Tragedy strikes and suddenly we wonder what God is doing. Will we survive? Will we be consumed by our difficulties? Will we make it through and can we trust Him? The answer is yes, but we may have to go through some very stormy times along the way.

As I listened to her words, a mental image flashed into my mind. I remembered how maritime sailors survived great storms. When they felt there was a serious threat of being washed overboard and out to sea, they bound themselves to the ship's mast so they would not be swept away. What are you bound to? Are you tied to your own ability to search out the best care for your son or daughter? Have you become so panicked that you can't sleep or rest for thinking of one more thing that could be done to help? Or have you just given up? You are weary, tired, and mentally exhausted. You need a Savior and there is only One. Jesus Christ came so that you would never have to face anything alone. To those who are hurting, He gives comfort. To those who are weary, He gives His own strength. And to those who feel like giving up, He lifts them up and covers them with His wings of rest and repose. You do not have to give up. You may need to take some time off, but not in order to run away from the responsibility God has given you. Instead, you may need time to draw near to Him and allow Him to minister His truth and mercy to your heart and mind. If you do run, make sure the running you do is into His great arms. Isolation is not the answer to your problems, but many times taking time to draw aside from the battle with God offers fresh hope, insight, encouragement, and renewal.

One of my favorite psalms is Psalm 91. In it, the Lord gives us words of comfort and hope and the ever-present reassurance that He will shelter and keep us during the stormy times of life:

He who dwells in the shelter of the Most High will abide in the shadow of the Almighty. I will say to the Lord, "My refuge and my fortress, my God, in whom I trust!" For it is He who delivers you from the snare of the trapper and from the deadly pestilence. He will cover you with His pinions, and under His wings you may seek refuge; His faithfulness is a shield and bulwark. You will not be afraid of the terror by night, or the arrow that flies by day. . . . For you have made the Lord, my refuge, even the Most High, your dwelling place. (vv. 1–5, 9 NASB)

CHAPTER 7

Fresh Hope

Daniel was in a very difficult spot, I thought as I looked at the artist's painting. The older woman who had asked me to drop by for a visit was intent on me seeing the illustration one more time before I left her house. Each of my visits before this one had ended in the same place: me standing in front of this old print. It was one that I had seen countless times in old churches and Sunday school buildings. But there I stood once again looking at the face of a man who, despite his situation, did not seem troubled at all. Was I missing the intent of the artist? I had not thought of it until this moment. "Do you see it, preacher?" Her question reflected a childlike eagerness as she waited for my answer.

I studied the scene and certainly saw things that could be pointed out. "The lions are up, not laying down," I replied, "and it is as if they are circling Daniel. But God is preventing them from attacking him." I knew I was right, but was I seeing what she saw?

"No, no, no," she said shaking her head. "Look at his face. He's looking up at the light! He is not concerned about what is going on behind him. His focus is set on one thing: God!" I looked again, and she was right. White light washed in from a hidden source and fell down all around the prophet. Daniel's face was turned upward. Instantly, I knew what the artist was depicting. The focus of Daniel's faith was not on his circumstances. It was on God. There was not a hint of worry on his face because he knew God loved him and the Lord was perfectly in control. This dear woman also understood that I was in a very difficult situation in my own life. It was her way of reminding me that there was only one way out of the darkness and that was to keep the eyes of my heart set on Jesus. Nothing else would work.

It is possible to be in a very difficult situation and have an abiding sense of peace within your heart. Even when trial and tragedy have taken their toll on your emotions, you can enter into a place of rest that God has reserved for those who have troubled hearts. It is a place you can go whenever you need fresh hope and understanding. Physically, Daniel may have been in a lions' den, but mentally, emotionally, and spiritually he was in the presence of God. Urgency and impending death circled him. Fear beckoned for his undivided attention, but he was focused only on God. What is the focus of your heart? When the doctor steps into your room or the police officer walks through the doorway, are you willing to lift the eyes of your heart to the Lord and allow Him to bathe your heart and emotions in His understanding love and care?

DON'T WASTE YOUR SORROWS

Most of us know that it is unwise to waste money. But I wonder how many people know just how unwise it is to waste suffering. Throughout this book, I have often said that God has a purpose for every trial we face. And yet we usually do not think about this at all or not until we have spent many white-knuckled moments in fearful expectation. Very few people, if any, would sign up to experience tragedy, even if they understood that there would be eternal gain involved. No one I know enjoys watching their child struggle, even when it is from peer pressure or moments of preteen insecurity. The fact is, we don't like to think about our children hurting even when we know that it will work out for their good.

A lot of people waste their sorrows by complaining and begging God to change or remove their circumstances. They want out of the difficulty, and they don't want to wait another minute. We see this played out over and over again in homes. We tell our children to do a certain thing and they ignore us, or unwillingly attempt to comply. We do the same thing to God. He disciplines us or allows us to face adversity to prepare us for greater blessings, and we either complain or beg Him to release us. We act as if we do not want to know what He is trying to teach us through the experience, and this is where the problem arises.

It is never God's will for you and me to experience suffering without profiting from it. But we must come to a point where we stop focusing on the difficulty from our perspective and begin to look at it through God's eyes. This is where we learn obedience and gain a greater sense of God's love for us. He doesn't want any of us to hurt, but He knows that it is a part of life, and therefore He is very determined to use the trial or tragedy for His honor and glory. At any point, we can resist Him. Many of us have seen people fight hard against God. I have heard a father say, "If He allows my son to die, then that's it! I'll never trust Him again." How arrogant and how sad this type of statement is. I understand what it feels like to lose someone you love greatly. I know the heartache that comes from getting up in the morning and wondering if life will ever be the same. But blaming God and, more than this, becoming bitter toward Him only plays straight into the devil's hand.

Satan wants us to give up. He has set up the scene with one thing in mind: tempt us into denying God and walking away from our faith—which is impossible to do. We never walk away from God's love because we are forever in His presence. We can turn our backs on Him and become involved in activities that are totally outside of His will, but we can never escape Him. He is everywhere, and He will never give up on us. Even when we throw our hands up and shout, "Quit!" He stands by knowing that we are hurting and waiting for us to turn back to Him. The heart that has grown cold to the things of God is a greater tragedy than anything we can witness.

After he had lost everything—his health, his children, and his home—Job's wife came to him with anger-drenched words: "Are you still holding on to your integrity? Curse God and die!" (Job 2:9 NIV). Job, however, would not buy into her sin-induced words. "You are talking like a foolish woman," he replied, "Shall we accept good from God, and not trouble?" The Bible goes on to say, "In all this, Job did not sin in what he said" (v. 10 NIV). It takes extreme faith to see beyond our troubling circumstances. And yet this is what He wants us to learn to do. It is what Job did, and it is the same thing that Daniel did. Neither one of these men acted to the extreme. They did exactly what faith in God had trained them to do—watch, wait, and obey.

Could Daniel have learned the lesson God wanted to teach him outside of time spent in the lions' den? Maybe. God can enlighten our hearts with His truth in different ways, but we would not have his story to read (Daniel 6). I would not have had the opportunity to stand in front of that old illustration and think about God's presence surrounding me even when it was not visible with human eyes. I'm convinced that Daniel's faith increased in ways that we cannot imagine. He may not have even realized what he was learning until after his release. That is usually the way faith develops. Tragedy, trial, or hardship comes and we have a choice. Either we can run to one friend and then another and lie awake for endless hours worrying about what will happen and how it will take place, or we can fall on our faces before God and ask Him to carry the burden that we are feeling.

As I got in my car that day after visiting the woman with the painting, I made a decision to trust the Lord with my problem and that no matter what happened in the future, I would get through this valley by keeping the eyes of my heart set on Him. This was an extremely important decision because even though I knew I had faith in God's ability, the trial was so severe that I was constantly thinking about many of the same things everyone considers: What would happen in the future? How would God work everything out for my good and His glory? And how could I help Him along the way? I was very happy to learn He really did not need my help as much as He wanted my fellowship and devotion.

When I committed myself to prayer and spending more time with Him and less mental time with my burden, the stress and pressure I had been feeling began to fade. Notice I said the stress and pressure lifted, because it was no longer the focus of my thoughts. The adversity remained, but I had changed, and you can too. God's plan for us and for the hurts we suffer is this: He wants to draw us to Himself. Job's odyssey ended in blessing, but it was not just a material blessing. It was an eternal blessing because Job, like Daniel, realized he was standing in the omniscient presence of Holy God. He said, "I have heard of You by the hearing of the ear; but now my eye sees You; therefore I retract, and I repent in dust and ashes" (Job 42:5, 6 NASB).

THE IMPORTANCE OF BEING IN GOD'S PRESENCE

God knows exactly what we need and when we need it. He knows when we are ready to hear His words of encouragement and when we are too caught up in our own thoughts of pain and disappointment. Every trial or pressure that God allows to touch our lives is given for a specific purpose and that is to shape us into His image. This is why we should never waste a failure or a season of suffering. If we allow Him to use it in our lives, then He will bring good out of it at some point. This is His promise to those who love Him and who have chosen to live their lives for Him. He tells us, "We know that God causes all things to work together for good to those who love God, to those who are called according to His purpose. For those whom He foreknew, He also predestined to become conformed to the image of His Son" (Rom. 8:28, 29 NASB). We hear this verse quoted a lot, but often the quote ends with verse 28. It feels good to think about God working everything together—no matter how harsh the trial is—for our good. It is difficult, however, to think about the responsibility that we have before the Lord. To discover the true meaning of this verse and others, you can't take it out of context and understand what God wants to say to you. You must read it surrounded by the accompanying verses. We gain a complete mental picture of God's words in this section of Scripture when we read:

> In the same way the Spirit also helps our weaknesses; for we do not
> know how to pray as we should, but the Spirit Himself intercedes

for us with groanings too deep for words; and He who searches the hearts knows what the mind of the Spirit is, because He intercedes for the saints according to the will of God. And we know that God causes all things to work together for good to those who love God, to those who are called according to His purpose. For those whom He foreknew, He also predestined to become conformed to the image of His Son. (vv. 8:26–29 NASB)

By reading God's Word this way, we suddenly discover that He is aware of our weaknesses. He has given us His Spirit, not only to pray for us, but also to intercede for us with "groanings" of love and sincere empathy. He knows all about us because He searches our hearts. Our way, as the psalmist reminded us in Psalm 139, is not hidden from God. He wrote:

My frame was not hidden from you when I was made in the secret place. When I was woven together in the depths of the earth, your eyes saw my unformed body. All the days ordained for me were written in your book before one of them came to be. How precious to me are your thoughts, O God! How vast is the sum of them! Were I to count them, they would outnumber the grains of sand. When I awake, I am still with you. (vv. 15–18 NIV)

Even before you took your first breath, God was aware of all that you would be given to experience throughout all the days of your life. He is aware of your troubled heart, but He is also aware of the way you need to walk through each trying moment.

Peter reminds us that suffering is for a season: "After you have suffered for a little while, the God of all grace, who called you to His eternal glory in Christ, will Himself perfect, confirm, strengthen and establish you" (1 Pet. 5:10 NASB). The psalm carries this thought one step further: "Weeping may last for the night, but a shout of joy comes in the morning" (30:5 NASB). It is okay if you cannot imagine enjoying a joyful moment, especially as you watch your child struggle with some form of pain. But God does set limits to the pain and suffering, and He also promises that we will experience joy and hope. Believers who transfer their anger, hurt, and frustration to God in prayer not only gain a new perspective of their situation, they also gain wisdom and insight into how to handle the difficulty. It is a win-win situation.

The closer we draw to God, the more we learn about His nature and plan. In the beginning a trial may appear devastating. However, as we spend time with Him in prayer, our hearts begin to change and we experience the purifying results that come from being in God's care. I have had people tell me that when their trial was over and all was settled, there was a part of them that missed the fellowship they had with God on this intense and deeper level. One woman told me how she felt as though she had drifted away from the Lord until she realized that she was perfectly in step with Him. "I felt such a sense of loss. When I was fighting depression, I woke up early every morning. I decided since I was up early, I would make the most of my time by taking my battle to the Lord in prayer. When the depression began to break apart, I began to sleep normally. One morning I woke up after my alarm went off and I knew things had changed. Later that day, I remember smiling over the fact that God had healed me. Suddenly, I missed Him terribly. And even though I do not want to become depressed again, those moments of darkness became a sweet memory to me because I relied so heavily on Him and not on myself. It was a wonderful way to live even though it was a very painful time."

The reason I know you and I can profit from suffering is because I have felt this in my own life. I have learned through suffering that the God of all mercy and grace is in control, even when my circumstances seem out of control. There is no such thing as uncontrollable suffering. God is in control of all things at all times. The apostle Paul reminds us, "No temptation has overtaken you but such as is common to man; and God is faithful, who will not allow you to be tempted beyond what you are able, but with the temptation will provide the way of escape also, so that you will be able to endure it" (1 Cor. 10:13 NASB). This means that every trial, heartache, or form of suffering—no matter what it is—has a limitation on it. And that limitation comes from God—the same God who loves us with an infinite love and is the God of all grace and mercy. He is merciful in His thoughts toward us. He doesn't turn away when we suffer; He is actively working on our behalf in ways we cannot see.

Many times, when suffering seems beyond our control, our response is, "God, I can't handle any more than this." The implication is, "Lord, you have 'twisted' this wrenching pain within me one too many times." God knows the limitation He has set, and if this is the way you feel, I want to encourage you not to give up. You may be standing right before a door of hope, release, and freedom from the burden you have carried for a long time. Don't give up; God knows how much you can take, and He will not stretch you beyond what you can endure. For some people, emotional pain is the worst. They would say that there is no physical pain that can compare to the pain of loss, anxiety, and fear. This certainly is true for those who have children who are hurting. We can be tempted to think, *If God really loves me, why would He allow this to happen?* The answer is because He loves us and trusts that we will surrender to His work in our lives. Even though we may feel out of control after the doctor tells us, "There is nothing more that I can do," remember, there is always something God can do!

YOU CAN GAIN FRESH HOPE

Sometimes He allows the suffering to continue. Sometimes He brings it to a quick halt. Sometimes you may mentally look down the road of suffering and think, *God, there is no end in sight. Please give me a sense of hope that I can hold on to.* He has told us, "I will not leave you as orphans; I will come to you" (John 14:18). While Jesus spoke these words to His disciples, they are words that contain a promise that we can claim. God never leaves us without hope. Our circumstances may not work out the way we planned or prayed they would, but God will help us through the difficulty, and then He will use the pain we have felt to encourage others along the way. Throughout the entire process, He never leaves us to battle the enemy's threat alone.

How do you gain fresh hope for the journey you have been given to travel?

Admit you have a need. The first step is crucial to the entire process. I have often thought, *I wonder if they really realize they are in a very difficult situation,* when people have left my office after a counseling session. Denial can help us process our pain and hurt in the early stages of any trauma. But there are people who live in a state of denial and this is what I'm talking about.

Perhaps you receive the news that your son has cancer. Immediately, your mind will go through several phases—shock, denial, anger, and acceptance. There could be more or less than these, but usually denial is in the mix. God understands that you may need time to work through your feelings of disbelief. Usually, He will set up the circumstances so you are forced to move toward acceptance. This takes place at a much faster pace when your heart is already turned toward Him. However, if you are still shaking your head and denying the reality of the problem three weeks after it has occurred, then you need a reality check fast. Denial can be very frightening, because the more you deny a problem exists, the more you will have to work to convince yourself that you are right.

Admit that you cannot make it through this trial without Him. I meet people all the time who refuse to admit their need for God.

They know the challenge is greater than their ability to handle it, and yet they keep trying to find a way to solve it without His involvement. When we have the God of the universe standing beside us, why would we turn to our own human reasoning? What would motivate us to look within ourselves when all we have is finite reasoning and a tainted view of life and reality?

Remember the lady whose son began having seizures? She told me that one of her first thoughts was, *How do I fix this?* But she knew she could not do it on her own. This was beyond her ability as a mother to heal. So she began her search for a doctor who could end her son's suffering, "At first, God was not the focus of our search. We turned to the doctors. Sure, we prayed, but we were asking for God to work through a physician. This is what He eventually did. After my son spent another year on medication, the doctors became convinced that they could remove the small marble-size tumor that was pressing against his brain. However by this time, God was no longer a casual consideration. He had become the central focus of our lives.

"While my husband and I wanted our son to be well, we also wanted God's will for his life. I didn't know how I would reconcile it if the operation did not work, but I was convinced God would show me. Just as we had prayed for years, God healed my son. The tumor was removed and the seizures stopped. Looking back, I have a single regret and that is this: I wish I had not waited so long to trust God. I wish I would have admitted my need and allowed Him to work instead of getting in His way." One of the exciting aspects of this story is the fact that in the end, she discovered what God wanted her to learn all along. He was trying to teach her to trust Him with her entire life—even her loved ones. How many of us have thought, *God, I surrender everything to you. You can have it all.* But deep inside, we secretly pray, *But please don't touch the life of my daughter, son, husband, or wife. I could not handle seeing them hurt.*

God is not up in heaven waiting for the right time to hurt or crush our hearts. He is a God of love, but because of the nature of our world, bad things do happen. When they do, we can either turn to the Lord with open heart and hands, or we can clinch our fists and close ourselves off from Him. I can tell you that the second choice is the most painful one you can make. If you have a son or daughter who is hurting, you need all the wisdom you can handle. And God will provide this, but first you need to admit there is a problem, and you need help.

Humble yourself before the Lord and be willing to surrender every area of your life to Him. Peter was a prince when it came to pride. That is until he surrendered his life to Christ. Even then, he had some issues that needed God's attention. However, after the crucifixion and his denial of Christ, things began to change. Peter saw himself partially through God's eyes, and he did not like what was there. The coming of the Holy Spirit and his full surrender to the Lord altered the way he lived his life to such a degree that he wrote First Peter to encourage new Christians living under dire persecution to trust God and not relinquish their faith. In other words, hold fast to what they had been taught and never stop believing in the goodness of God, regardless of their circumstances. The one thing they could cling to was Jesus Christ—the risen Lord, who conquered death. Once you have faced suffering and come through it believing and experiencing the healing power of God, you are never the same. Added to this experience in Peter's life was the fact that he saw the risen Savior and experienced the coming of the Holy Spirit. He wrote,

> Humble yourselves under the mighty hand of God, that He may exalt you at the proper time, casting all your anxiety on Him, because He cares for you. Be of sober spirit, be on the alert. Your adversary, the devil, prowls around like a roaring lion, seeking someone to devour. But resist him, firm in your faith, knowing that the same experiences of suffering are being accomplished by your brethren who are in the world. After you have suffered for a little while, the God of all grace, who called you to His eternal glory in Christ, will Himself perfect, confirm, strengthen and establish you. (1 Pet. 5:6–10 NASB)

Peter understood the way you feel. He knew the ache your heart contains. And he is saying, "Don't give up. Don't give in. Don't turn away from the One—the only One—who can strengthen, encourage, and lift you up." Notice that he did not say that God would take away all the pain and grief. There are some things in life that we must endure all the way to the end. When we place our trust in Christ, He will change the situation or He will give us the strength we need to get through it.

Surrender to the idea of His peace and not your retaliation. As long as you insist on fighting back, you are really not in a position to accept what God has to say or do. I always know when a person is open to the will of God because he or she will say something like, "I just want God's will for my life or the life of my loved one." Or they may say, "I just want to draw closer to Him so I can hear His voice. I think if I can hear Him say that everything will be okay, then I will be able to go on." God is still speaking to us, but the key to surrender and to hearing His voice is stillness. We must become still and surrendered enough in our hearts and minds so we can hear what He has to say. As long as we are trying to champion our own cause and find an answer, we risk not hearing His voice. I'm not saying that we should become relaxed in our thinking. We need to be keen when dealing with doctors and medical professionals. However, there is a sense of stillness and rest that we can experience in God's presence that is separated from the noise of this world. When we are spiritually and emotionally tethered to Him, we are much more likely to hear His voice of guidance, love, and encouragement.

Ask Him to show you how to walk each day trusting Him and not your feelings. Thoughts of worry and fear can blind us to the hope that God has for us to enjoy. When we are immersed in thoughts of doubt and anxiety, we cannot hear—with our hearts—the truth of God's Word spoken to us. It is like walking through a thick cloud. We may be moving, but we don't know where we are going because we are frightened and pessimistic about the future. Think about those who play sports. Maybe a baseball player starts out like a champion. He is hitting a home run every other game, helping his team to move up in the standings. Then a sport's writer decides to print a column questioning how long his "run" will continue, especially since it seems that he is not a natural home-run hitter. Suddenly, the player starts striking out. Every time he comes to bat, he thinks, *Everyone thinks I'm not a natural. I don't really believe it either.* He swings at the first ball that is thrown across the plate and misses. And so it goes.

Satan knows exactly what to whisper in your ear to tempt you into believing his lie instead of God's truth. I have seen people who were quite healthy become sick because they suddenly caved into worry. The mind is a powerful thing. While we want to be realistic, we also need to recognize that the enemy will stop at nothing to prevent us from trusting God, achieving His goals, and looking to Him for a solution to our trials and troubles. Bottom line: The enemy wants you to believe the worst, grow anxious and worried, and dismiss God's power in your life. I explained this to a young father who was struggling with depression over his daughter's illness. I encouraged him to get back into God's Word by reading the Psalms and asking the Lord to speak to him through prayer. He balked at my suggestion and said, "But you don't understand. The doctors have told me there is no hope." This is when we need God's Word hidden away in our hearts—when it appears there is no hope.

God has something to say to us even when standing at the bedside of a loved one who is dying. He never intended for us to walk through a valley alone, and yet this is what Satan desires for us—isolation, fear, rejection, and loneliness. With everything in me, I want to encourage you not to give into feelings of doubt or fear. "Trust in the LORD with all your heart and do not lean on your own understanding. In all your ways acknowledge Him, and He will make your paths straight" (Prov. 3:5, 6 NASB).

Open your heart to being used by God. One of the best ways to move past any hurt is to stay active. You may need to take time to allow God to bring His healing work in your heart, but then ask Him to get you back into the flow of life, even if that flow is centered on a recovery program for your child or an extended stay in the hospital. You can be an encouragement to others who are going through similar circumstances. This is the foundational truth and the success of any support group, which the Lord may lead you to join. In times of trouble, isolation does not encourage recovery. At times, all of us need to be alone in order to rest, become refreshed, and discern God's truth. As you open yourself up to others, something amazing happens. You will begin to sense your energy returning. God created us to comfort one another, to listen, and to be a support. These are all characteristics of His nature and nurturing care toward us.

Years ago I asked my mother why she continued to visit nursing homes on a regular basis. I told her, "Mom, you don't need to do this anymore." But she was very deliberate in her response to me: "Yes, I know that, but I want to be used by God for as long as He will allow it." There was something about visiting people who were hurting that energized her. I'm sure she never told the ones she visited about the difficulties she had during her life. She didn't have to say a word. Most of us know when someone understands the hurt we are feeling. We can see it in their eyes—compassion and empathy is a language that everyone understands.

The one thing that I noticed about my mother's life was the incredible sense of hope she maintained, because she knew that nothing was too difficult for God. You may be in the middle of a horrendous situation and wonder if you will ever feel hopeful again. The answer is always yes when He is involved. He calls us to a life of holiness, purity, and service. God may be testing your faith during this difficult time, but He is also preparing you to be a minister of hope to others who need to know that there is light at the end of the tunnel.

CHAPTER 8

Solving Your Problems
Through Prayer

"I never thought I would have this type of pain." The father looked up at me through eyes that were filled with tears. I confess that I wanted to join him and cry too. It seemed that the heartache he bore was more than the average person could handle. Yet I knew it was not too much for him as long as he stayed connected with God. "I thought that once I became a Christian, life would not be so difficult. I don't know what I was thinking, but if this is the way it is going to be, I don't know what I will do." I sensed that a lot of what he was expressing came from feelings of sheer fear—ones that all of us have felt at one time or the other.

The man who brought his son to Jesus understood the feelings of fear and hopelessness. Matthew records the scene this way:

A man came up to Jesus, falling on his knees before Him and saying, "Lord, have mercy on my son, for he is a lunatic and is very ill; for he often falls into the fire and often into the water. I brought him to Your disciples, and they could not cure him." And Jesus answered and said, "You unbelieving and perverted generation, how long shall I be with you? How long shall I put up with you? Bring him here to Me."

And Jesus rebuked him, and the demon came out of him, and the boy was cured at once. Then the disciples came to Jesus privately and said, "Why could we not drive it out?" And He said to them, "Because of the littleness of your faith; for truly I say to you, if you have faith the size of a mustard seed, you will say to this mountain, 'Move from here to there,' and it will move; and nothing will be impossible to you. ['But this kind does not go out except by prayer and fasting.']" (17:14–21 NASB)

It is obvious that Jesus is disappointed by the poor faith of His disciples. He points out to them that it is not just their waning faith that is the problem but also the faith of an entire generation. In other words, this lack of faith in God was characteristic of the culture and society. Much like today, people enjoy hearing about a miracle, but they do little to entreat God to work on their behalf. This father was desperate. He had faith enough to believe that Christ's disciples could heal his son. They had been very successful; then this moment challenged their ability to trust God. Why? They had become careless. A string of successes due to the fact that Jesus had given them power to heal left them feeling as though they could do anything—they could heal and cast out demons. The catch, however, was this: They could not do anything in their own strength.

Later, they wanted to know what had gone wrong. For one, they had acted in their own strength. Something had changed within their thoughts where they began to see their role as almost magic, which was a popular thought in their culture. There were many false prophets who practiced magic. While the disciples did not practice magic, the source of their faith had shifted just enough from God to themselves to render their work ineffective. We see this played out in our own lives each day. The moment we disregard who our source of strength is, we become ineffective in our ministry and work.

Jesus took command of the situation by healing the man's son and then telling the disciples what they had done wrong. "Because of the littleness of your faith; for truly I say to you, if you have faith the size of a mustard seed, you will say to this mountain, 'Move from here to there,' and it will move." The word "littleness" in this context means poor. The object of their faith was not necessarily God. There was a lot of their own ability mixed into the equation, and the results were not good. The power they needed to do kingdom miracles was not their own. It was derived from faith in God. Jesus went on to tell them privately, "This kind does not go out except by prayer and fasting." Prayer is the key to healing because it signals that our hearts are God's. In times of prayer, He teaches us to focus on Himself and nothing else. Problems may continue, but when we are in close communion with God, we have a tremendous advantage over every difficulty we encounter.

The disciples, though called and empowered by Christ, needed to remember that it is God's power through them that heals, strengthens, and empowers. A long line of successes easily can be followed by failure when we become too sure of ourselves and not aware of who is responsible for our lives, gifts, and talents. Here is an even greater truth: prayer cannot change God's mind; however, it does change us. He knows what He is going to do and how He will solve our problems. When we pray, we are demonstrating our faith and trust in Him. We may begin with a list of things that we want done a certain way. We ask for healing—something that He longs to do, especially if it fits His will. We seek His intervention in our lives and the lives of those we love. "Lord, please remove this suffering." "Help the medication to work." "Take away the pain." There may be a host of other requests, but as we trust Him and pray each day, something amazing begins to happen. We may continue to think about our circumstances, but we begin to see them through eyes of faith in Christ. Then over time, our focus shifts from being fixed on earthbound matters to ones that are reflective of Him: His personal love for me, His will for my life, His purpose for the struggle in my child's life or in my own.

You may be reading this book and wonder how God can possibly solve your problem. Your son or daughter may have left home. Many times, emotional distress does not involve physical pain. We may wonder why God has not answered our cries for help. But we never need to worry. He always answers prayer according to His timing and will and not ours. One of the most important questions we can ask ourselves is this: "Am I willing to abide with God and wait for His solution?" If we go to God with a preconceived notion of what the solution is, then we have already decided how He should answer our prayer.

In 2 Chronicles, King Jehoshaphat and the people of Judah found themselves in a very precarious spot. Trouble with their enemies had been brewing for a while, but it was not until an attack was about to happen that the king became very worried. In fact, he became "afraid and turned his attention to seek the LORD, and proclaimed a fast throughout all Judah" (20:3 NASB). Suddenly with death staring them in the face, God had their full attention. What had been a casual activity suddenly became urgent. All of Judah came together to seek help from the Lord. "Jehoshaphat stood in the assembly of Judah and Jerusalem, in the house of the LORD before the new court, and he said, 'O LORD, the God of our fathers, are You not God in the heavens? And are You not ruler over all the kingdoms of the nations? Power and might are in Your hand so that no one can stand against You'" (vv. 5, 6 NASB). He goes on to remind God and the people about the way the Lord had worked in the past. Jehoshaphat's principle motive was to bring the people together in prayer. Everyone wanted to be there, and everyone cried out to God for help and deliverance from their enemies.

There are several principles you need to learn considering prayer:

God wants us to turn to Him. The Lord was waiting for the nation of Judah to ask for His intervention. He knew the enemy was too great for them to handle. They needed Him, but they also had to turn to Him and make their need known. It may seem very natural to pick up the telephone and call a friend. But for a Christian, the most natural thing we can do is to turn to God in prayer. It is in times of prayer that He reminds us that we are not alone and we are not powerless because of His life within us. Prayer can instantly lower our level of anxiety and fear, especially when we need to make a decision in times of crisis.

We need to accept His goodness, forgiveness and unconditional love. When we do we can leave every feeling of guilt and fear at the foot of His cross. Just because someone is going through a difficult time does not mean he or she has sinned. Remember, at some point, each one of us will face adversity. It is a fact of life. But God has promised to use the trials of life to draw us closer to Himself. He wants us to know that when the storms of life hit, He will be there with us and He won't ever leave. Feelings of false guilt and inadequacy can block our communication with God and with others. But prayer and the study of His Word break down the barriers that could be used by the enemy to prevent us from knowing God and experiencing His love, hope, and freedom from the bondage of sin and shame.

God is interested in your problems. The Lord was totally invested in the care and future of Judah. He cares when we are hurting and discouraged. He doesn't want us to feel left out, overlooked, or forgotten. In times of crisis, He knows we can be tempted to feel like giving up. But if we will remain open to the work of the Holy Spirit, we will sense His encouragement. Prayer coupled with God's Word are our greatest weapons of faith. We may be frantic for an immediate answer to our prayers, but God is more interested in the level of our faith. He will send the right answer at the right time, but until He does, His call to us is the same one He gave the disciples: "Abide in Me" (John 15:4 NASB). The wonderful thing about the nation of Judah is that they took God at His Word. The next morning when they marched into battle, Jehoshaphat placed the choir up front instead of the fighting men. He believed God would deliver His people and this is exactly what happened, but first, they prayed.

Nothing is too big for Him to handle. It was an army of thousands that had gathered against God's people—the odds were not in Judah's favor. In fact, defeat seemed imminent. We have made this point in earlier chapters, but it bears repeating: Nothing is too great for God to handle (Gen. 18:14; Jer. 32:17). Nothing is beyond His reach—no experience, no tragedy, no trial. He is over all things, and when we take time to go to Him in prayer, we have the matchless, awesome opportunity to address holy, righteous God and know that He will listen to every word we speak simply because He loves us and only wants the very best for us.

God wants us to seek His face through prayer. This is exactly what the nation of Judah did. Instead of fortifying the walls around their city, they sought God to fortify their hearts through prayer. God created us for fellowship with Him. Prayer is the way we accomplish this. It teaches us how to commune with Him and creates an atmosphere of contentment and peace within our hearts. Jesus was in the boat with the disciples that stormy night on the Sea of Galilee (Matt. 8:23–27). They became frantic and never considered that they were in the presence of the Son of God. They were safe in His care and yet instead of moving closer to Him, they frantically struggled with oars and sails trying to keep their boat from sinking. God was with them and He is with us, but we must set aside our oars for a period of time and pray. When we do, He will command our seas to become quiet and still. We can face any trial because we know Jesus Christ will not abandon us.

God provides for your situation. The Lord was moved to action at the sound of Judah's prayers. They marched in the battle the next day, but they never considered fighting because they knew God had a plan and He would implement it. As we pray, His Spirit opens our hearts to godly truth. I never limit my time in prayer to voicing my needs to the Lord. I read His Word, study His truth, repeat His promises to Him, and meditate on His goodness. I also take time to be still and quiet before Him. I listen in reverent silence for God's leading. Before I know it, He brings a passage of Scripture to mind that addresses my specific need. Or He may choose to make me sensitive to something I'm reading in His Word that applies perfectly to my situation. What happens if I get up and have not heard from God? My level of trust only deepens. I know that His silence means that He is watching and knows when I need to hear from Him. I may need guidance in a certain area. Many times He will provide it in advance, and other times He waits until later when the need is very urgent. Regardless of the timing, He is never late. He is always perfectly on time.

Prayer leads to praise, and this is where we discover God's greatest blessings. One of the first things we notice in 2 Chronicles 20 is that the singers were chosen to go first into battle. And they didn't just hum a little tune. They sang boldly to the Lord and proclaimed His faithfulness and unbridled love for them: "[Jehoshaphat] appointed those who sang to the LORD and those who praised Him in holy attire, as they went out before the army and said, 'Give thanks to the LORD, for His lovingkindness is everlasting'" (v. 21 NASB).

When you pray, praise God for who He is, what He has done in your life, and what He will do in your situation. Thank Him even though you may not see the evidence of His work, and trust that He is moving and He is bringing deliverance to you.

When they began singing and praising, the LORD set ambushes against the sons of Ammon, Moab and Mount Seir, who had come against Judah; so they were routed. For the sons of Ammon and Moab rose up against the inhabitants of Mount Seir destroying them completely; and when they had finished with the inhabitants of Seir, they helped to destroy one another. When Judah came to the lookout of the wilderness, they looked

toward the multitude, and behold, they were corpses lying on
the ground, and no one had escaped. (vv. 22–24 NASB)

Judah never had to raise a sword, shoot a single arrow, or
run the length of the battlefield. God heard the nation's prayers
and words of praise and He boldly answered.

Here are three personal points that I have found helpful
concerning prayer:

Pray with a God-centered heart. Throughout this chapter, I
have stressed the need to focus on God in prayer. The trouble
comes in the tendency that most of us have to become fretful. It
is as if we think God does not know what has happened. He
wants us to come to Him immediately seeking His wisdom,
guidance, and protection. But He understands our need to tell
Him all about the problem, our feelings, our regrets, our fears,
our struggle with guilt, and our feelings of discouragement. One
woman whose daughter had left for college fought back tears as
she explained how out of control she felt. "I just want to go with
her and make sure she has everything she needs." I smiled
because just as God is aware of our desires and needs, He also is
totally aware of the ones our children have. Our challenge is to
let go of our need to control and allow Him to work His will in
our life and the lives of our children.

Pray with humility. As we read earlier, Peter wrote, "Humble
yourselves under the mighty hand of God, that He may exalt
you at the proper time, casting all your anxiety on Him, because
He cares for you" (1 Pet. 5:6, 7 NASB). There are people who

falsely believe that if they appear humble, they will be considered weak. But this is not the case. When we humble ourselves before God in prayer, we position ourselves for great blessing. I'm not writing about material wealth; I'm talking about the blessed assurance that comes from spending time in God's presence as a result of humble prayer. However, if we continue to believe that we must be in control and deny Him His rightful place as Lord over all, then we are the ones who miss out. The position of prayer is very important. I have heard people say, "I'm not going to get down on my knees and pray." Yet this is the very position that God calls us to assume. How many times does the Bible record the prayers of men and women who "bowed down" before Him? Praying on our knees is a signal that we truly honor and love Him, and that we view Him as Lord of our lives.

You may pray on your knees every single time. However, there is something about getting down on our faces before God, confessing our needs, our inadequacy, and our desire to be what He wants us to be that changes everything. This is really what the people of Judah did in their hearts. They fasted and prayed at home, but then they gathered in God's presence and humbled themselves before Him. There is no way God would fail to answer prayers prayed in this way. If you are struggling and feel as though no one understands, take time to get alone with the Lord. If you physically can, get down on your knees or lie down on the floor with His Word open before you and just take time to be quiet and worship Him. Sing softly and tell Him your concerns. Listen for

His goodness to be revealed and refuse to tell Him what you think should happen or what you are going to do next. Just humble yourself, let go, and let God love you and be Lord of all in your life. If you will do this, you will be amazed at how your enemy will disappear before you. Sickness and disease may linger, but these will no longer have the power to pursue or conquer you.

Pray with a desire to become more like Christ and not just to find an answer to your problems. God motivates us to pray through time spent in adversity. There is no doubt that when the heat is turned up, we start to look for solutions. Many times we are quick to turn to Him. Other times we don't. We just keep doing what we have done for far too long. I watch people struggle and continue to struggle until finally, they realize there is a way through the valley and it begins with prayer. I always tell them that while God is interested in our difficulties, His greater interest is in how we handle our circumstances. In times of heartache and trouble, do we really want to know what He desires for us to learn? Are we only interested in getting through the ordeal, or are we willing to pace ourselves according to His timing.

Prayer has an ability to bring us right in line with God's will. It is a doorway into His glorious presence where we find unspeakable hope for even the most hopeless situation. I believe that once a person has tasted of God's goodness in prayer, he or she will never want to drift away. That person will return over and over again—staying longer and drinking deeper of His truth and intimate love.

The psalmist wrote,

How lovely are Your dwelling places, O LORD of hosts! My soul longed and even yearned for the courts of the LORD; my heart and my flesh sing for joy to the living God. The bird also has found a house, and the swallow a nest for herself, where she may lay her young, even Your altars, O LORD of hosts, my King and my God. How blessed are those who dwell in Your house! They are ever praising You. Selah. How blessed is the man whose strength is in You, in whose heart are the highways to Zion! Passing through the valley of Baca [weeping] they make it a spring. . . . Every one of them appears before God in Zion. O LORD God of hosts, hear my prayer; give ear, O God of Jacob! Selah. . . . For the LORD God is a sun and shield; the LORD gives grace and glory; no good thing does He withhold from those who walk uprightly. . . . How blessed is the man who trusts in You! (84:1–8, 11, 12 NASB)

In humility before Almighty God, in submission to Him, humbling yourself before Him, bring your heart and sorrow to Him in prayer. Then as you bow down in faith, give everything you have to Him through prayer and know that the God of all mercy and grace will take care of all that concerns you and the ones you love.